CANADIANS
IN THE
SUMMER OLYMPICS

**Canada's Athletes, Victories, Records,
Controversies, Firsts and Weird Facts**

J. Alexander Poulton

OVER
TIME
BOOKS

The Publisher: OverTime Books is an imprint of Éditions de la
Montagne Verte

Library and Archives Canada Cataloguing in Publication

Poulton, J. Alexander (Jay Alexander), 1977–
    Canadians at the Summer Olympics : Canada's athletes, victo-
ries, records, controversies, firsts and weird facts / J. Alexander
Poulton.

Includes bibliographical references.
ISBN 13: 978-1-897277-33-1
ISBN 10: 1-897277-33-4

    1. Athletes—Canada—Biography. 2. Olympics—Participation,
Canadian. 3. Olympics—Biography. 4. Paralympics. I. Title.

GV697.A1P68 2008   796.48092'271   C2008-901696-3

Project Director: J. Alexander Poulton
Project Editor: Brian Crane
Production: Alexander Luthor, Jodene Draven
Cover Image: Courtesy of Popperfoto/Getty Images

We acknowledge the financial support of the Government of
Canada through the Book Publishing Industry Development
Program for our publishing activities.

PC: P5

Canadian   Patrimoine
Heritage   canadien

Contents

Dedication

To my great uncle Harry Poulton who competed in the doubles 1000-metre canoeing event with Douglas Bennett at the 1948 Olympics in London and came in fourth.

The Tale of Canada's First Olympian

When George Washington Orton was born in 1873, Canada was only in its sixth year of existence, barely aware of itself as a nation. At the 1900 Olympics in Paris, when George Orton won the gold medal in the 2500-metre steeplechase and the bronze in the 400-metre hurdles, it gave Canadians a sense of pride. It earned recognition for what it truly meant to be Canadian.

Growing up in Strathroy, Ontario, George Orton's life took a strange twist of fate when he was temporarily paralyzed by a fall in his childhood. To overcome his paralysis, his father had him run behind the family's horse-drawn buggy wherever they went, earning him the local nickname of "the boy who never walked." George Orton kept on running so much that his father figured he had best enter him into a local competition lest people think the boy was different. Orton won that competition and continued to run while attending the University of Toronto and later at the University of Pennsylvania.

Running for his American alma mater, Orton won more American national championships than any previous runners. He won races across North America and in the United Kingdom as one of the top middle distance runners in the mile, two-mile and steeplechase events. These distinctions, despite the rules concerning U.S. citizenship, earned Orton a place on the American team travelling across the Atlantic to Paris for the 1900 Olympic Games. When the athletes finally arrived in Paris after a long trip across the Atlantic by boat, they found that the French had not laid out a racetrack! They had simply marked out an area in the grass at the Paris horseracing circuit. It wasn't exactly the perfect conditions for running an Olympic race. There were several dips and mounds in the course, and a large grove of trees near the finish line obstructed the spectators' view. Fans would interfere with competitors in their attempts to get a better view.

The French sparked further controversy when they scheduled several of the events to take place on Sunday. This outraged several of the more religious U.S. competitors , and they dropped out of their events. Orton saw no reason to give up his chance at an Olympic medal, so he joined

Walter Tewksbury of the United States and Henry Tauzin of France as the only three competitors in the 400-metre hurdles. It was Orton's first event, and he came in last. But this happened to be good enough for a bronze medal! It was Canada's first-ever Olympic medal.

Just one hour later, Orton returned to the "so-called" track for the 2500-metre steeplechase. Given Orton's history of middle distance running, it was clear from the list of competitors that he was the favourite with Great Britain's Sidney Robinson as his only major competition.

At the sound of the gun, Orton took off with the rest of the pack and held slightly back of the leaders for the majority of the race. As the group approached the last uphill climb before the grove of trees, Orton decided to make his move. Spectators saw Orton start to pass a few runners before disappearing into the trees. Then suddenly, he reappeared alone at the front of the pack on the other side. He won the race easily—and in world record time—before collapsing in exhaustion at the finish line.

After his Olympic victories, George Orton retired from competitive athletics and became the track coach at the University of Pennsylvania. He died in 1958.

He was posthumously entered into Canada's Sports Hall of Fame in 1977 as Canada's first medal winner at the Olympic Games.

Over the next 108 years Canada sent over 4000 of its best and brightest following the tradition set by George Orton. They strive to be the best in the world for one shining moment. Not all of the athletes are lucky enough to wear a medal around their necks, but they are lucky enough to represent our nation's flag with pride, honour and dignity. It is those athletes to whom I dedicate this book.

Introduction

He who says it can't be done is usually interrupted by someone doing it

–Anonymous

Canadian amateur athletes have attended the Summer Olympics since 1900, showing everyone that they are among the best in the world. Over the years Canada has had its ups and downs, winning medals in some of the most exciting moments in sports and losing in some of the most touching and humbling ways. There have been moments that made the nation hold their heads high and moments that have made Canadians hang their heads in shame. But if there is one constant that has held throughout the years that Canadians have been competing, it is that they have always given their very best. In victory or defeat, they have carried themselves in a way that has shaped the country and added to the essence of what it means to be truly Canadian.

Canadian Olympians have not always had the corporate sponsorship or the same government support that other modern athletes receive. For the 1900, 1904 and the 1906 Olympics, Canada did not even have an official team, forcing Canadians like Etienne Desmarteau and William Sherring to make their own way to the Olympics, paying for travel, room and board. Canada's William Sherring raised the money to get on a boat to travel to the Olympics in Athens, Greece in 1906 but once there had to work in the train station in Athens to pay for a room and a ticket back to Canada when the Olympics ended. How things have changed!

Canada's history at the Summer Olympic begins with George Orton, although it wasn't discovered until years later that he was actually Canadian. Orton was born and raised in Canada but had moved to the United States to further his studies. Since Canada was not officially sending a team to the 1900 Paris, France Games, Orton simply tagged along with his American friends. He ended up winning one gold and one silver medal. For a long time the Americans claimed Orton's medals as their own (and they still do by the way), but it wasn't until many years later that Orton actual citizenship was discovered making him the first Canadian to have ever won an Olympic medal. For years, it was believed that

Montreal police officer Etienne Desmarteau had captured Canada's first medal when he won the gold in the 56-pound hammer throw. But George Orton's gold in the 3000-metre steeplechase and bronze in the 400-metre hurdles the first of Canada's 242-total medals at the Olympic Games.

Throughout the years, there have been many Canadians that have inspired. More recently a few Canadians have tarnished what it means to represent their country. When you hear the name Ben Johnson, you don't think Olympic bronze medalist at the 1984 Summer Games. You think the 1988 steroid scandal that rocked Canadian amateur sports. Millions across Canada watched proudly as Ben Johnson beat longtime American rival Carl Lewis in world record time at the 1988 Olympics in Seoul, Korea, in the biggest event of the Games, the 100-meter sprint. The entire nation rejoiced at having won the most prestigious medal in the Olympics, but just a few days later, it was discovered our national hero had taken performance-enhancing drugs. Ben Johnson had cheated. The collective disappointments Canadians felt was palpable. The ripples of that discovery put the spotlight on another of Canada's athletes and had many wondering if the entire Canadian sports program had been tainted. Just a few days after it was discovered Ben Johnson had cheated, hurdler Mark McKoy suddenly dropped out of his event and returned to Canada. He later admitted to using drugs to improve his chances at the games. But just when it seemed Canada could not get any lower, other athletes stood up and won back our pride.

Although he wasn't born in Canada, Lennox Lewis, won the boxing gold in the super heavyweight category, clean and fair just days after the Ben Johnson scandal. Having broken his right thumb in one of the early bouts, it didn't look promising that Lewis would be able to finish the Olympics let alone win a medal. But with help from his trainer and a lot of tape around his thumb, Lewis developed a new style of fighting that relied more on his left jab than his right hand knockout punch. The new style proved effective and was probably the reason he was able to bring home Canada's first boxing gold medal since Horace "Lefty" Gwynne's win at the 1932 Los Angeles Games.

Canadian athletes have provided the Olympics with moments of sheer joy, inspiration and an example of the meaning of sportsmanship. Canadian sailor Lawrence Lemieux was on his way to winning a medal in the Finn class of sailing at the 1988 Olympics in Seoul, Korea, when he noticed that another competitor's boat had capsized. Two sailors inside where injured and in danger of drowning. He had a split second to choose between his Olympic dream and the lives of two men. For Lemieux the choice was an easy one. In the middle of his race he turned his boat away from the finish line and straight for the drowning men. He might have lost his chance at gold, but two men are alive today because of what he did, something that is far more precious than any medal.

The story of synchronized swimmer Sylvie Frechette is one of great courage and an inspirational story for every Olympic athlete. Just a few days before realizing her dream of competing in the Olympics, Sylvie Frechette returned home from practice hoping to relax for the rest of the evening with her fiancé, but instead she came home to find that he had committed suicide. This was just six days before she flew to Barcelona for the opening ceremonies of the 1992 Olympic Games. Pushing herself forward and using the pain in her life as inspiration, Sylvie Frechette put on one of the most memorable performances from the 1992 Games clearly earning the gold medal for her efforts. But a judge's error caused her to receive only silver. After some protests by Canadian officials, however, one year later Sylvie Frechette stood at the center of the Montreal Forum and received the gold medal she had deserved all along.

These and hundreds more stories of Canadian athletes' personal triumphs and defeats are a part of the history of the Olympic Games. Battling personal demons or the ticking of the stop watch, our athletes will continue to provide us with incredible stories as we look toward the future to the next time we gather before the best in the world and show them what Canada is truly made of.

Chapter One

Track and Field

The Infamous Sprinter

In just 9.79 seconds, Ben Johnson went from being another unrecognizable Canadian athlete to one of the most famous faces in the world and the holder of the distinguished title "World's Fastest Human."

It is easy to remember the pride and joy the nation felt when their fellow countryman defeated some of the fastest human beings in the world at the 1988 Seoul Olympics premiere event, the 100-metre sprint. It is equally easy to recall the shame the entire nation felt just three days later when it was revealed that our gold medallist and world record holder was found to have the synthetic anabolic steroid Stanozolol is his system.

The rise of Ben Johnson as a major competitor in athletics really began four years before the

1988 Seoul Olympics at the 1984 Olympic Games in Los Angeles in the 100-metre sprint final.

Johnson was well aware that he would have to run the race of his life in order to beat the favourite, American Carl Lewis. Rather than showing a mutual respect for each other, the two athletes constantly battled on the track and in the media. Lewis' arrogance was unparalleled, while Johnson held the conviction and confidence of the man in second place. Despite what either man said before the race, it didn't really matter on that race day in 1984 when their drama played out in a burst of energy that lasted 10 seconds or less.

Cameras flashed and 100,000 spectators held their collective breath as Johnson and Lewis approached the starting blocks for the 100-metre sprint final. Johnson approached the blocks, crouched down and knew he had to run the race of his life to best Lewis. The starter raised his pistol, but just a fraction of a second before the crack of the gun broke the silence in the stadium, Johnson jumped out of the blocks. Johnson later admitted that he had done this purposely to throw Lewis off his game. Unfortunately, Johnson's little piece of strategy didn't work. When the starter pistol rang out a second time, Lewis got the early jump out on the field and ended up winning gold. Johnson ran his way to a respectable third place.

Coming so close to beating his rival was not good enough, and with a renewed sense of purpose, Johnson focused on his training. By the time the 1987 World Championships in Rome rolled around, Johnson had beaten Lewis four times at international track events but of lesser importance. With the world's eyes now on Rome for the premiere event at the World Championships, Johnson would have to prove himself once again, despite having already shown that he was capable of being the best.

The day of the big race, all eyes were on Ben Johnson and Carl Lewis. The 100-metre sprint was the premiere event of the World Championships, and everyone wanted to see these two titans of sport do battle on the track. As much as Carl Lewis tried to dismiss Johnson before the race, he surely thought, as he entered the blocks, that he could lose the prestigious title of "World's Fastest Man" to the cocky Canadian.

With a loud crack, the sprinters took off toward the finish line. Johnson got an early jump on the field, turned on the afterburners and never looked back. Johnson ran so fast he set a new world sprint record of 9.83, leaving Carl Lewis behind to ponder what had happened.

After Rome, Johnson became athletics' number one celebrity. Product endorsements poured in; journalists called for countless interviews; and it seemed everyone had an award to give out. As much as Johnson welcomed the fame, it also had its darker side.

"I didn't know what it was going to be like," said Johnson. "Now I'm successful, and I'm paying for it."

Things were made even worse for Johnson when Lewis, in an attempt to explain away his defeat in Rome, publicly accused the 100-metre gold medallist of using performance-enhancing drugs.

During a controversial and often replayed interview with the BBC, Lewis publicly lamented his fate: "There are gold medallists at this meet who are on drugs. That (100-metre) race will be looked at for many years, for more reasons than one."

Johnson was vindicated of all charges of using drugs during the World Championships in Rome after submitting to post-race drug tests, but the allegations of cheating continued to follow him, tarnishing his victory. Johnson chose to take the high road in the whole affair.

"When Carl Lewis was winning everything, I never said a word against him. And when the next guy comes along and beats me, I won't complain about that either."

The public verbal jabs set up an epic rivalry that would play out on the track at the 1988 Olympics in Seoul, Korea.

Through the dark tunnel leading out to the Olympic Stadium, Ben Johnson, Carl Lewis and the other participants in the 100-metre final, were hit with the brilliant rays of sunshine on that warm Saturday afternoon in Seoul. The roar of the 70,000 spectators gathered to see history in the making was deafening.

With the entire world watching, Johnson was keenly aware of the pressure he was under, and he knew if he could win just this one race, he would achieve immortality. He needed to win at any cost.

"The gold medal is something people remember. It is something no one can ever take away from you," said Johnson prophetically in a pre-race interview.

All the allegations, all the hype and all the trash talking, didn't matter now. It came down to the next 100 metres: lifelong glory achieved in a matter of a few unforgettable seconds.

The starter's pistol sounded. The first few steps, Ben Johnson held the pack at bay. From there it was simply a matter of finishing the race. With the gold medal already around his neck, and only a few strides to the finish, Johnson triumphantly pointed one finger to the sky as he crossed the line with a new world record time of 9.79 seconds.

Johnson grabbed a Canadian flag from one of the spectators and proudly waved his nation's emblem for the world to see. But the pride the nation felt at having the fastest man in the world lasted only three days.

On September 27, 1988, Ben Johnson received a call from Carol Anne Letheren, *chef de mission* of Canada's delegation to the Summer Olympics, informing him that the second drug test he had taken had tested positive for the banned anabolic steroid stanozolol. "Ben," she said, "we love you, but you're guilty."

For a brief moment Ben Johnson was the best in the world, with a gold medal around his neck and the title of the world's fastest human. Yet as dramatic as his rise to fame was, his downfall was even more spectacular and garnered him even more attention. In the beginning Johnson denied taking any drugs, but even his agent Glen

Calkins admitted glumly, "God is going to have to come out of the heavens to fix this one."

In a world that idolizes and rewards its athletes with untold wealth and fame, winning had become everything, and Ben Johnson became the poster boy for a system gone wrong. In 1984 before he began taking drugs, Johnson was only good enough to finish in 3rd place behind rival Carl Lewis. In his mind, performance-enhancing drugs were the only way to achieve the recognition he had wanted so badly. And he got it. But Johnson was recognized for all the wrong reasons.

Just one week after winning the gold medal and capturing the imagination of the world, Ben Johnson was sitting in the witness stand at the federal judicial inquiry before Mr. Justice Charles Dubin of the Ontario Supreme Court, finally admitting what everyone else knew to be true. He had knowingly taken steroids.

"I lied," said Johnson at the federal inquiry, "and I was ashamed for my family and friends and the kids who looked up to me and the Canadian athletes who want to be in my position."

Johnson attempted a comeback but once again tested positive for high levels of testosterone at a 1993 race in Montréal. As a result, the International Association of Athletics Foundation

(IAAF) finally banned him from competition for life.

As sad as the story of Ben Johnson was it serves today as a warning to younger athletes of the dangers of drug use in sports. A lesson Ben Johnson would surely agree with.

The Famous Sprinter

The ghost of Ben Johnson's positive drug test at the 1988 Olympics cast a long, dark shadow over the Canadian track and field program. But then one man came along, and in a blur of speed and sheer human will, brought a sense of self-respect and pride back to the Maple Leaf.

Unlike other modern Olympians, Donovan Bailey did not start a serious career in athletics until just two years before his appearance at the 1996 Centennial Summer Olympics in Atlanta, Georgia. He emigrated from Manchester, Jamaica, to Canada at the age of 13 with his mother. They decided to settle in Oakville, Ontario. In high school Bailey was a natural at track and field but preferred to devote of his time to basketball. Sports were fun, but his tough Jamaican mother instilled in him a strong sense of pride and commitment to education. After getting his business administration degree from Sheridan College, Bailey entered the world of high finance and became a successful stockbroker.

While watching the Canadian National Track and Field Championships in 1990, Bailey realized that some of the athletes were people he used to beat on a regular basis in high school. Bailey always believed in meeting goals and facing new challenges. He took up track and field part-time in 1991 and eventually found his way onto the Canadian National Team. Bailey might have had the raw talent, but he was missing a coach who could make him a true star.

In 1993 Donovan Bailey's running career would change drastically when he met legendary track and field coach Don Pfaff. With his keen sense for talent, Pfaff recognized Bailey's drive for success, but he knew that the young sprinter would need a lot of work to become the best in the world. Pfaff insisted that Bailey join him down at his training facilities at Louisiana State University to work out his bad mental and physical habits.

Within the span of a single year, Pfaff had molded the brash young stockbroker from Canada into one of the fastest men on the planet. At the 1995 World Championships, Bailey won the 100-metre sprint gold medal and helped his teammates win the 4x100-metre sprint relay, proving to the world that he was one of the top athletes in his sport and that anyone that wanted to challenge him would have to be at their best. While others spent their entire lives training for these events, Bailey had become the best in the world in less than four years.

Winning the World Championships is an amazing accomplishment, but to win gold at the Olympics is to achieve immortality. The 1996 Summer Olympics in Atlanta, Georgia would be Bailey's stage.

For eight years, Canada had lived under the shadow of the Ben Johnson steroid scandal. Now they pinned their collective hopes on Bailey's shoulders. In 10 seconds, Bailey could wipe away the shame that had been hanging over the Canadian Olympic program, a fact he was well aware of as he stepped into the blocks for the finals of the 100-metre sprint.

Lined up beside Bailey were the world's fastest men, all vying for the same title, all capable of winning the gold. Among them were Trinidad's Ato Boldon, Namibia's Frank Fredericks. Bailey's fiercest competition was reigning Olympic gold medallist, England's Linford Christie.

The pride of their nations, each man wanted to burst out of the blocks to get that extra millisecond jump on the competition. Olympic champion Linford Christie was the first to jump the starting gun and was charged with one false start. Tensions were high, and on the next attempt, Trinidad's Ato Boldon jumped out ahead of starting gun. Sometimes sprinters false start on purpose in order to throw off their opponents' timing, but

Donovan Bailey remained calm and focused on the job ahead. For the third time, the sprinters took their marks, got set and bang! Linford Christie jumped the gun for the second time. With a second false start, Christie was disqualified. The drama of the moment increased when Christie refused to accept the official's judgment and would not leave the track. But his protests fell on deaf ears, and once Christie was off the track, the runners returned to the starting line.

Taking his mark for the fourth time, Donovan Bailey took a deep breath and stared down the 100-metre track. The race official's disembodied voice called out over the speaker. "Runners, on your mark. Get Set." Then the loud crack of the starter pistol sounded, and the seven remaining runners leapt forward, muscles flexing, lungs pounding and hearts racing toward glory.

Things did not look promising for Bailey in the first 40 metres. He was in the middle of the pack, and it looked like he couldn't pull even. But Bailey was a notoriously slow starter and always ran best in the last 50 metres. As expected, by the 50-metre mark, Bailey turned on the jets, pulled ahead of Ato Boldon and Frank Fredericks and never looked back. Bailey had brought the gold medal home to Canada. More importantly, he restored the sense of pride that was taken away eight years earlier. And he did it in world record time! As Bailey crossed the finish line, his face contorted into a scream of pure happiness. As he took his victory lap around the stadium waving a large Canadian flag, he knew that he had his place in the history books, the immortality that every athlete dreams of.

Bailey's Olympic successes did not end with his 100-metre gold medal. Bailey had another shot at glory as part of the Canadian men 4x100 relay team. This was the greatest assemblage of runners Canada had put together in its history. Starting off the race was Robert Esmie, who had shaved the message "Blast Off" in his hair as a message to the other runners he would leave in his wake. Glenroy Gilbert would take the baton for the second part of the race, followed by Bruny Surin who was Canada's best at running the corners. Bailey would anchor the race, giving Canada its best shot over the final 100 metres.

From the moment the starter pistol sounded, the Canadian men took the lead and never looked back. By the time Bailey got the baton for the final leg of the race he could almost have jogged to the finish line. Had he not raised his hand in triumph during the last 15 metres, the team might have broken the world record. They just missed it by .29 seconds.

Winning the relay gold secured Donovan Bailey's position as one of the greatest runners Canada has ever produced.

In 1988, Canadian had a national hero for just three days; in 1996 they got a national hero for life.

Donovan Bailey continues to be a force in the community with his many charitable initiatives and remains close to the sport that has given him so much.

1996 100-metre Olympic Sprint
Final Standings

Athlete	Country	Time	Finish
Donovan Bailey	Canada	9.84 sec	1st Place (Gold Medal)
Frank Fredericks	Namibia	9.89 sec	2nd Place (Silver Medal)
Ato Boldon	Trinidad & Tobago	9.90 sec	3rd Place (Bronze Medal)
Dennis Mitchell	United States	9.99 sec	4th Place
Mike Marsh	United States	10.00 sec	5th Place
Davidson Ezinwa	Nigeria	10.14 sec	6th Place
Michael Green	Jamaica	10.16 sec	7th Place
Linford Christie	Great Britain	N/A	Disqualified

The World Champion's
Olympic Heartbreaker

Before the 2004 Summer Olympics in Athens, Greece, odds makers had an easy time selecting who would be the favourite to win the women's 100-metre hurdles.

Canada's Perdita Felicien had been tearing up the track and field circuit since she laced up her first pair of sneakers for her high school track team in Pickering, Ontario. Taking inspiration from track superstars Bruny Surin and Donovan Bailey, Felicien dedicated herself completely to the world of track and field, working out constantly and training every moment she could spare. The commitment to her craft began to pay off at a young age. After she won the Province of Ontario's Hurdling Championship in 1997, she knew that her talents could take her far. After a number of brilliant performances at various tournaments, she was offered an athletic scholarship from the American University of Illinois. It was at the University of Illinois that Felicien met up with her coach, Gary Winckler, and began her meteoric rise to the top of the amateur track and field world. Eventually, she was being compared to the legendary American track star Gail Devers.

After receiving countless awards and victories at the University level, Felicien began competing on the international stage at the 2003 World Championships in Athletics in Paris, France.

In her small university world, Perdita Felicien was a famous star. On the world scene, she was a relative unknown going into the World Championships despite her long list of victories, including a silver medal at the Pan American Games. Felicien could have easily won the gold medal at those games had she not felt a few nervous butterflies going up against the best athletes in the world. For the World Championships in Paris, Felicien had decided to turn things around.

In the final race, Felicien burst from the blocks in one of her best starts and never looked back on her competition. She won the race in a Canadian record of 12.53 seconds, winning Canada's first female world gold medal in track and field history. After the race, Felicien was beaming with confidence.

"I'm not scared of these girls anymore," she said of her competition. "I hope they are scared of me."

Felicien followed up her 2003 gold medal with a much-anticipated showdown with American Gail Devers at the 2004 World Indoor Championships in Budapest, Hungary, in the finals of the 60-metre hurdle. Felicien was anxious to race against Devers since many people had claimed that her gold medal in Paris had been won by "default" because Devers had not been on the line.

The pressure was on. Felicien described the race in her journal page on the Track & Field News website:

With the start of the gun in the final I got out quite slowly. I was so thankful for the sound of the gun (false start pistol) as I cleared the first hurdle. That false start was my second chance. I walked back to the line and literally said out loud to myself, "If you are trying to get a medal you have to get out better than that, this is your second chance, you better take it." I was on the money the next time around and knew at hurdle one how much better my start was. The entire length of the way I felt Gail (Devers) and that we were running with each other step for step. I tried to pull away—but couldn't. I knew during the race that no matter what happened when we came to the finish line I was running faster that I had ever before. With hurdle five approaching I must admit I expected the world champion in the 60 metres to fly past me, since her flat speed amongst sprint hurdlers is incomparable. But something happened after I cleared the last barrier, I saw the line and mustered all the strength and raw speed I had in me and surged for it.

Felicien had done what no one expected her to do. She had defeated the legendary Gail Devers and had earned the respect she had so long deserved. The excitement was palpable in her words as she looked forward to racing at the Olympics: "I take that as a sign of formidable races and incredible challenges to come in my event this summer—and I can't wait!"

With nothing but high hopes and dreams of gold in mind Perdita Felicien walked into the 2004 Summer Olympics in Athens, Greece, as the favourite to take home the gold medal in the women's 100-metre hurdles and possibly more. She had already proven that she could handle the best by defeating Gail Devers. All that was left to do was to have another good race.

All of Canada had their eyes on the young hurdler from Pickering, Ontario, as she prepared herself before the start of the finals of the 100-metre hurdles. She had easily made her way through the preliminary rounds and was looking calm but focused as she approached the line for the start of the race.

Back in Pickering, Ontario, family and friends gathered around the television at her parent's home with fingers crossed and blood pulsing to watch her bring home the gold. It seemed to most that it was almost a sure thing that Felicien would win the race seeing as her biggest rival had to pull out of the competition in the semi-finals because of a calf injury. All she had to do was get to the finish line.

When the starter pistol sounded, Felicien leapt off the line and had the early lead on the pack within the first few steps. At the first hurdle, disaster struck. Her foot caught the top of the hurdle sending her sprawling to the ground and careening into the lane of Russian Irina Shevchenko. Through the tears in her eyes, Felicien watched the other hurdlers run down the track to the finish line where she was supposed to be.

Back home in Pickering, Ontario, at her parents' home, there was silence around the television as the broadcasters tried to explain what had happened. The family's hearts dropped when they saw Perdita being interviewed by the CBC's Scott Oake. "This is my worst nightmare come true," said Felicien. Unable to hold back her emotions, she stared directly at the camera and offered an apology to all those cheering her on back home and around the world. "I'm sorry I let you down."

After so many promises and with the expectations of a nation on her shoulders Perdita Felicien ended her Olympic dreams in tragedy. But ever the optimist she admitted in a post-race interview that she would be back at the Olympics in 2008 in Beijing "with bells on" to bring home the gold medal that she felt she let slip through her fingers. With the 2008 Olympics fast approaching, an entire nation will have their fingers crossed as she takes the starting line.

For the record: U.S. hurdler Joanna Hayes crossed the line first with an Olympic record time of 12.37. Second place went to Ukrainian Olena Krasovska with a time of 12.45, and third place went to Melissa Morrison of the U.S who took the bronze with a time of 12.56 seconds.

Triathlon Gold

The gruelling pace, the blazing heat, the freezing water, the burning muscles, every part of your being telling you to stop and rest with each step—this is just a small sample of the pains that the Olympic triathlete must face in order to have a chance at Olympic glory.

The triathlon was added as an Olympic sport in 1904, but Canadians have never faired very well. Individually Canada has done okay for itself in swimming, cycling and running events, but with the three events combined, our athletes have never seemed to be able to make it up onto the podium. Our greatest hope came at the 2000 Olympics in Sydney, Australia, and bore the name of Simon Whitfield.

Ranked 21st overall in the world, Whitfield wasn't given much hope of winning the Olympic event. Many world-class athletes placed well ahead of him before the start of the Sydney Olympics. Whitfield was just happy to attend.

"My goal had always been to get to the Olympic Games as a medal contender," he said in the book *Heroes in Our Midst*. "So on September 12, 2000, when I arrived in the athletes' village in Sydney, Australia, I felt I had accomplished my goal."

On race day Whitfield packed in among 51 other competitors on the edge of Sydney Harbour ready to dive into the chilly waters. (They have been known to contain sharks by the way). When the gun sounded, Whitfield dove into the water and began his 1.5-kilometre swim. He emerged from the water in 28th place knowing that he would have to rely on his background in cycling and running to catch the leaders. Luckily, the 27 other competitors in front of him where in a tight pack, and by the time he made his way through the cycling transition zone, he was within 38 seconds of the Australian leader Craig Walton.

On the bike, Whitfield quickly worked off the chill from the water under the glaring Australian sun. During the 6.6-kilometre circuit that ran through downtown Sydney, Whitfield made his way through the pack and began to eke out a tiny lead from the group in the rear. With only a few kilometres to go in the race, he found himself in ninth place and within striking distance of the top three. If he was going to have a chance at an Olympic medal, this was it. He almost lost that chance when a rider just a few metres ahead of him miscalculated a turn and crashed, taking down several riders. Thinking fast, Whitfield slammed on the breaks and came to a stop just in time to avoid adding to the tangle of bodies and bikes.

While he was lucky to avoid the crash, having to stop in the middle of the race put him in 27th place. By the time he reached the running portion of the race, he was 70 seconds behind the leader. Whitfield was left with just 10 kilometres to make up the distance. Things weren't looking good for the Canadian, but as he later explained, "I believed that the winner of the Olympic triathlon would be whoever could put all the preparation together and was relaxed and confident. But ultimately it would come down to who wanted it most."

Strongest on his feet, Whitfield quickly began to gain ground on the leaders, clearly believing that he wanted the gold the most. Close to the end of the race, he found himself in fourth place and closing in on the top three. He passed the third place runner, and then blew by exhausted French runner Olivier Marceau for second place. First place runner German Stephan Vuckovic was in Whitfield's sights.

Vuckovic made an early attempt to distance himself from Whitfield, sprinting toward the finish line that lay just 600 metres ahead, but his early jump for the finish line used up any reserve power he had, leaving Whitfield with a golden opportunity. Finding the energy from somewhere deep inside, Whitfield sprinted down the last few hundred metres blowing by the exhausted German. At the finish line of the most challenging race in the Olympics, Whitfield leapt across the line, breaking the Sydney 2000 tape as Canada's first-ever triathlon gold medallist.

At the medal ceremony as the Canadian national anthem blared over the speakers, Whitfield bowed his head and began to cry. He had realized his dreams and had pulled out the race of his life at just the right time.

The Redeemed Athlete

Born in Guyana and raised in England, Mark McKoy came to Canada when he was a teenager. He burst out onto the international athletics scene in the early 1980s, winning a gold medal in the 110-metre hurdles at the 1982 Commonwealth Games. He continued his strong showing on the international scene representing Canada at the world championships and finally participating in his first Olympics in 1984 in Los Angeles. There he placed 4th in the 110-metre hurdles. Just 24 years of age when he competed at the 1984 Olympics, McKoy seemed destined to have gold in his future. But over the next few years, his world would be turned completely upside down.

His fall from grace began just before the 1988 Olympics in Seoul, Korea. At 28 years old, McKoy was one of the older competitors in track and field and more and more he was losing ground to the younger players. He began to realize that he needed an edge over the competition if he wanted to win a gold medal. His solution was something he would come to regret later.

At the 1988 Seoul Olympics, McKoy breezed his way through the preliminaries in 110-metre hurdles but was taken out in the final when he timed his jumps badly over several hurdles and ended up finishing in seventh place. The performance was a big disappointment for McKoy, but he had another chance at redemption as one of the runners in the 4x100 metre relay. Before the start of the event, it was discovered that his fellow Canadian runner Ben Johnson had tested positive for steroids and had been stripped of his medal. Upon learning of Johnson's disgrace, McKoy suddenly packed his bags and jumped on a plane out of Korea. Rumours immediately began to circulate that McKoy was using steroids as well, and a short while later, McKoy confirmed the rumours that he had taken performance-enhancing drugs. For his indiscretion he was suspended from international competition for two years.

During his two-year absence, McKoy refocused his efforts on his training and made a return to competition at the 1991 World Championships where he finished in 4th place in the 110-metre hurdles. Although he had moved to Austria in 1990, he was still a Canadian citizen and was able to run again for Canada at the 1992 Olympics in Barcelona in the 110-metre hurdles.

McKoy proved to the world that he could run a clean race and still be competitive as he made his way through the preliminary rounds and into the finals. His toughest competition in the finals were Tony Dees of the United States, Tony Jarrett of Great Britain and his good friend and training partner Colin Jackson of Wales.

At the crack of the starter pistol, McKoy leapt out of the blocks, and by the time he reached the second hurdle, he was clearly out in front of the pack. With just one hurdle left to clear, it appeared that McKoy had the gold wrapped up, but he timed his jump badly and stumbled just before the finish. Luckily, McKoy had enough of a lead on the second place runner Tony Dees to finish the race in first place with a time of 13.12 seconds. He had his gold medal and his proof to the world that he could be a champion without any help. On his victory lap around the track, he wrapped himself in a Canadian flag given to him by a 20-year old Canadian attending Olympic Youth Camp. McKoy had his redemption.

The Incredible Harry Jerome

At one time he was the fastest man in the world, but most Canadians don't even know he existed. Harry Jerome's story is one, as are those of most of the athletes in this book, of overcoming incredible odds. Jerome faced down racism, doubts, injury and public scrutiny to become one of the most revered athletes in Canadian track and field history.

Born in Prince Albert, Saskatchewan, in 1940, Harry Winston Jerome, son of a railway porter, was given his middle name Winston because his father admired the British Prime Minister Winston Churchill for his strength and adversity in the face of insurmountable odds. The Jerome family picked up and moved to Vancouver when Harry was just 12 years old. At his new school, he fell in love with the game of baseball and was one of the best players on his North Vancouver High School team. But when the track coach noticed Jerome's speedy base running, he convinced him that his future was in track and field.

Never second-guess a coach's instinct. In his final year in high school, and only a short while after joining the track team, Jerome broke Canadian Percy Williams's 31-year-old record in the 220-yard sprint at the District High School Championship.

In 1959, Jerome was accepted at the University of Oregon. He studied on an athletic scholarship and continued his meteoric rise to the top of the athletics world.

Harry Jerome became an international name when in 1959, at only 18 years of age, he equalled the world record in the 100-metre sprint while competing in a track meet in Saskatoon. That record had been set by Germany's Armin Hary at 10 seconds flat. Suddenly, the world spotlight was cast on this shy black kid from rural Canada. At first he didn't know how to handle the pressure that came with success.

Harry Jerome got the call in 1960 to represent Canada in the 100-metre sprint at the Olympics in Rome, Italy. It was a dream come true for Jerome who had for so long wanted to prove himself capable of greatness. The son of a railway porter would finally have the chance to show to the world what he was made of. Unfortunately, on the day of the race, luck was not on his side.

Jerome was Canada's brightest hope in the 100-metre sprint at the Rome Olympics. He had already established himself as one of the favourites with his incredible record-tying run just one year earlier, and in the preliminary rounds at the Games, he finished at the top of the list.

Then came the semi-finals. Members of the Canadian sports media expected Jerome to come home with at least a silver medal since the only real competition in the race was fellow world record holder Armin Hary of Germany. All of Canada was watching, and Jerome felt every bit of pressure, much to his dismay.

Jerome burst out of the blocks at the sound of the starter pistol and had the early lead in the race through about the first 40 metres. Then out of blue, Jerome's face contorted with pain as he grabbed for his leg. Wincing with pain in the middle of the track, all Harry Jerome could do was to watch as the other runners sprinted to the finish line, jealous that they were living out his dreams. Rather than finding support from the Canadian media for his noble efforts, Jerome was crucified in newspapers and on the radio.

Sportswriters had built up the 100-metre sprint for weeks before the games, creating the expectation that Jerome would return to Canada the conquering hero with a gold medal around his neck. When he pulled up lame halfway through the race, those same writers who once praised his athleticism now berated him for caving under the pressure and accused him of being a quitter. Reporters demonized Jerome in part because the young runner avoided press conferences and interviews. He thereby only compounded the mystery and speculation as to why he pulled out of the race.

"Canada's Chance for Gold Medal Goes Limp as Jerome Pulls up Lame in Semi-final," screamed the headline in the *Toronto Telegram*. The article's author, Andy O'Brien, was less than kind to Harry's plight. "Of course, the unpopular Jerome could hardly have expected a sympathetic press anyway," wrote O'Brien sarcastically. "Luckily, he was the only one of our 99 competitors who failed to win respect." Another *Toronto Telegram* writer was more open in his contempt of Jerome. "Jerome was sulking before he started," wrote Ted Reeve. "And after the alleged leg ailment, he should have been put on the next boat home."

The attention however was brief, and Jerome returned to his school. After recovering from his injuries, he was back on the track getting into competition form.

Once healthy, Harry Jerome was tearing up the track for the university team and winning most races he competed in, but he had yet to prove himself on an international stage. Although he was calm under pressure, the fact that he did not finish in the 100-metre sprint at the 1960 Olympics continued to bother him, and he wanted a shot at redemption. He was hoping that it would come at the 1962 Commonwealth Games in Perth, Australia. But he again pulled up lame with a torn left thigh muscle. Fearing another incident with the Canadian press, Jerome was quarantined away from all journalists and quickly flown back to his hometown of Vancouver. The journalists came to the same conclusion they had in Rome and accused Jerome of quitting. As a man of colour during a tumultuous time in North America, Jerome constantly felt targeted and discriminated against. His avoidance of the media was simply a product of the environment he lived in, and he did not want to give the media any more ammunition. Jerome just wanted time alone to heal his injuries and chose not to deal with the media at all.

Doctors were not optimistic that he would compete, let alone, walk again. After a lengthy and difficult surgery, however, they changed their original diagnosis and told Harry that, after recovering, he could attempt to go back to the track.

After more than a year off, Harry Jerome returned to training and got himself back into competitive form just in time for the 1964 Olympics in Tokyo, Japan.

The finals for the 100 metres took place on an exceptionally hot mid-October day in Tokyo. Canada's best, Harry Jerome was up against speedy Cuban Enrique Figuerola Camue and American Melvin Pender. It was a tough heat, but Jerome had a slight advantage considering that Pender tore a rib muscle in the semi-final and would be racing with the handicap. Jerome' biggest obstacle was the American sprinter Bob Hayes. The two runners were the pre-race favourites for the gold medal, both sharing the record in the 100-yard dash.

The highly anticipated final was initially delayed because cinders on the track had been torn up in one of the previous races. After the grounds crews fixed the problem, the runners took their marks and at the sound of the pistol they were off. Jerome, Camue and Hayes matched each others' steps for about the first 20 metres, then with a sudden burst of raw power, the plucky American Bob Hayes pulled ahead of the pack and never looked back finishing the race in 10 seconds flat. Jerome and Camue both finished with a time of 10.2 seconds. Camue was awarded second place and the silver medal because he out-leaned the Canadian at the tape.

The once vitriolic press was now Harry Jerome's best friend.

"Sprinter Harry Jerome—Canada's Comeback Kid," bellowed the headline of the *Toronto Star*'s Jack Sullivan's article on the bronze medal win. He continued the praise in his article stating, "One of the greatest comeback stories in modern Olympics track history has been written at the National Stadium by Harry Jerome of Vancouver, supposed to be washed up two years ago." Harry Jerome had redeemed himself and at the same time relieved himself of the immense pressure of winning at the Olympics.

Even former Canadian Prime Minister John George Diefenbaker sent a congratulatory telegram, "Congratulations to you who have shown great courage in facing difficulties."

Harry continued his success on the track until his final appearance at the Olympics in 1968 in Mexico City. Jerome easily made it into the finals of the 100-metre sprint, but at the age of 28 he was one of the oldest athletes in the final. With Mexico City positioned at an altitude of more than 2000 metres above sea level, the cards were stacked against the Canadian runner. However, under these conditions he ran one of the best races of his career finishing in a time of 10.1 seconds. It was only good for seventh place. The American Jimmy Hines took the gold medal with a record-breaking time of 9.9 seconds. Harry

Jerome hung up his running shoes after those Olympics.

After his retirement Jerome continued to be active in the sporting world. He was tragically taken away too early when he suffered a brain seizure and died. He was 42 years old.

The Story of Tom Longboat

There is a common thread that runs through the lives of most great athletes as they work their way to the top. Their paths begin with hours of training, personal sacrifice and emotional strain. Add a few moments of doubt and failure, then after years of waiting, they finally get their glorious moment in the sun, a triumph over insurmountable odds. It is the stuff that legends are made of and what the Olympics are all about. However, this is not how the story of Tom Longboat begins, for he started at the very top and slowly worked his way to the bottom.

Born in 1887, on the Six Nations of the Grand River Indian Reserve near Brantford, Ontario, Longboat spent much of his youth working on a local farm. It was tough, manual labour, but by the age of 19, it helped give him great strength and stamina. Eventually, those days on the farm began to bore him, and a chance meeting gave him a possible way off the farm.

Another resident on the reserve, Bill Davis, told Longboat about a race being held in Hamilton. Davis, a one-time second place finisher in the Boston Marathon, pushed Longboat to try it out. Longboat, eager for something different, decided to give it a try and signed up for the 1906 edition of the Around-the-Bay Race.

Having never had any long-distance running experience, Longboat walked into the race wearing a cotton bathing suit and a pair of rubber sneakers. He surprised everyone in attendance with the ease of his stride, and he easily won the race beating the second place finisher by a full three minutes. He narrowly missed the course record by 42 seconds.

Seeing this amazing runner, the West End YMCA of Toronto asked Longboat to represent them at the 1907 running of the Boston Marathon. The premiere event on the running circuit, it attracted some of the best runners from North America and the world.

With only one race under his belt, Tom Longboat was confident that he could pull off a win in one of the most gruelling marathons. Much of the marathon's 24.5-mile course was uphill, and worse, on April 19, Longboat and the other 126 runners had to battle cold temperatures, snow, rain and the dreaded slush. None of that seemed to faze Longboat, who won the race in a record 2 hours, 24 minutes and 24 seconds. The record stood for four years and was only broken after the course was made easier.

The strange thing about Tom Longboat was that he never trained. His coaches had tried to get him to practice before races, but he always had the same answer. "I never trained before, so why should I now?" His logic seemed sound as long as he kept winning races.

When it came time for the 1908 Olympics in London, England, Tom Longboat was the first to jump at the chance to represent his country. All of Canada was behind their "Bronze Mercury," as the papers were calling him, and expectations were high that he would return with a gold medal around his neck. But the Olympic marathon would be his most challenging to date. At 42 kilometres (26 miles) it was, by far, the longest distance Longboat had ever attempted. It was the classic distance that a Greek soldier had covered in 490 BC while running from the city of Marathon to Athens with news of victory. After delivering his news, the messenger collapsed and died from exhaustion. The Olympic run would not be much kinder on Longboat.

It was an unusually hot, humid day in London as the runners prepared for the start of the race. With the sun blazing down from on high, Longboat took one last look into the air, breathed deep and, at the sound of the pistol, began running.

Longboat was out at the front straight from the start and set a furious pace. A quarter way through the race, many runners fell out from trying to keep pace with Longboat. But then around the 28-kilometre mark, Longboat began to look tired. He started to slow down. The sun and heat were doing their damage. Soon Longboat had to stop, as the sun and the humidity became too much for him. Crowds lining the streets watched in disbelief as Longboat had to quit the race and be driven into the stadium for medical attention. Canadians could not believe that the great Tom Longboat had lost the race. Worse, he did not even finish.

After the disappointment at the Olympics, Longboat turned professional and began a lucrative career running in various races around North America. But when the money began to pour in, Longboat's running started to suffer. After giving up halfway through a high-profile race against some former Olympic champions, Longboat career was on its way down.

When World War I broke out, Longboat enlisted as a private with the 180th Sportsmen's Battalion. After the war, Longboat returned to Canada but could not find solid work. He drifted from job to job eventually ending up as a garbage man in Toronto. After retiring in 1944, he returned to the Six Nations Reserve. He died five years later of pneumonia.

Canada's Bronze Master

Born into a wealthy upper class family in British Guyana, Phil Edwards enjoyed a comfortable life in his native country. In the 1920s, Edwards and his family decided to make a change and moved to New York to start a new life. Young Phil Edwards had shown great promise as a runner and would not get the training he needed in his native country. New York University had a reputable athletics program, and it seemed the perfect fit for Edwards. For a time things were promising as Edwards excelled in his studies and set several college records in middle-distance running events along the way. Edwards quickly established himself as someone who could compete on an international level and possibly at the Olympics. New York provided the perfect place for Edwards to realize his dreams of becoming a doctor, but he could not further his running career with the American national team. To realize his full aspirations, he would need to move to a country with a British connection.

Canada was the perfect fit. But the transition wasn't as smooth as he would have liked. In his native country of British Guyana, his family and he enjoyed a certain level of status in society, but in Canada at the time, feelings toward black people were less than welcoming. Edwards had difficulty adapting to the cultural shift. To keep the pressures of racism from ruining his opportunities, Edwards focused on his training and made the 1928 Canadian Olympic track and field team.

Phil Edwards started off his Olympic career as part of the Canadian men's 4x100-metre relay team. Edwards helped teammates James Ball, Stanley Glover and Alexander Wilson to a bronze medal. The team received little recognition that year given fellow countryman Percy Williams's double gold performance, but Edwards had put his foot in the door. He would return for the 1932 Olympics to earn the respect he had so long deserved.

At the 1932 Los Angeles games, Edwards was at his physical best. He blazed through to the finals in the 800-metre, the 1500-metre and the 4x100-metre relay. He won a bronze medal in each event. At the 1928 Olympics, he had been relegated to the statistics page in the newspaper for his bronze medal performance, but this time around he finally received the attention he deserved. The praise began to come his way.

"Phil Edwards was one of my favourite people in life," said 1932 Canadian high jump gold medallist Duncan McNaughton. "One of the finest human beings I ever met. He studied medicine at

McGill, had been Phi Beta Kappa at New York University and put up a damn good show in every Olympics in which he competed."

After winning four bronze medals in just two Olympics, Phil Edwards wanted one more chance at gold. He was getting older, but he was still in top shape and believed he could compete with the best in the world.

With a solid reputation and four Olympic bronze medals to his name, Edwards was named to be the Canada representative at the 1936 Games in Nazi Germany. Personally Edwards wanted to prove that he could still compete with the best in the world, but this Olympic Games also gave him a chance to show the hosts of the Games that their theories of Aryan racial superiority were nothing but fantasy.

Edwards made it into the final of the 1500-metre race and looked to be in contention for the gold but could not hold on in the last few hundred metres losing the gold to Jack Lovelock of New Zealand. Edwards had to settle for his fifth and final bronze.

On his way back to Canada, Phil Edwards and 50 other members of the Canadian team stopped in a London, England hotel to recharge before making the long trip back home. After proudly representing his country in the most racist nation in history, Edwards had to endure the insult of being refused a hotel room in that progressive city.

Insulted by the treatment of their captain, all 50 members of the Canadian Olympic team packed up their bags and followed Edwards to the next hotel.

Given the nickname, "Man of Bronze" for his five bronze medals, Phil Edwards was Canada's most prolific Olympic medal winner until he was joined by Clara Hughes and Marc Gagnon both with five Olympic medals and then ultimately surpassed by Cindy Klassen who won six medals in two consecutive winter Olympics.

Both of Edward's dreams had come true in the end: he had five Olympic medals and a doctorate in medicine from McGill University. For all his achievements in Canadian sports history he was posthumously named to Canada's Sports Hall of Fame in 1997.

Hilda's Strange Olympic Controversy

Canada' Hilda Strike won silver at the 1932 Olympics in Los Angeles, but 50 years later she found out, in one of the strangest moments in Olympic history, that she had deserved the gold all this time.

Growing up in the Montréal area, Hilda Strike played many sports as a young woman, but it was as a sprinter where the young Strike truly excelled. At the Canadian National athletics championship Strike easily won the right to represent her country at the upcoming 1932 Olympics in Los Angeles. She was the Canadian champion and the female athlete of the year, but on the international circuit not many gave the innocent-looking Canadian much of a chance. At 5-feet 4-inches and weighing in at just 105 pounds, Strike was rather tiny competition when compared with favourites like Poland's Stella Walsh (born Stanislawa Walasiewicz), who measured at 5-feet 10-inches and weighed only 155 pounds.

Competition for the 100-metre gold medal would be fierce. The odds makers were giving the odds to Stella Walsh because she held the world record in the event. (She was the first woman to break the 12-second mark in the 100-metre.) No one figured Canada's diminutive Hilda Strike would be a factor in the race.

Strike approached the blocks, stared down the line, and knew she would have to have the race of her life in order to make it to the podium. When the pistol sounded, Hilda broke out so fast that by the time she had reached the 30-metre mark, she had put a good distance between her and second-place runner Stella Walsh. At 60 metres, Strike could almost taste victory, but just as the gold seemed within reach, Walsh began to pull even.

The long powerful legs of Poland's Stella Walsh proved to be the difference in the race. In the last 5 metres, she pulled ahead of Strike and took home the gold medal for her country.

For Strike, it was far from a crushing defeat. The race marked her personal best time in the 100-metre sprint at 11.9 seconds, beating her old Canadian record of 12.2 seconds. She was proud of her silver medal. Her country was proud of her too. Hilda Strike returned to Canada an Olympic Champion, and as the years passed, memories of that race faded into the background. Hilda married and had kids but always stayed close to the sports she loved and that had given her so much. The story might have ended there had it not been for one of the strangest moments in post-Olympic history.

The gold medallist in the 1932 Olympic 100-metre women's sprint, Stella Walsh, lived her life, as did Hilda Strike, staying close to the sports she loved. After World War II ended, she decided to make Cleveland, Ohio, her permanent place of residence, and she was briefly married to boxer Neil Olson. All aspects of her life seemed perfectly normal until one day while shopping down at the local grocery store she was killed by a stray bullet during an armed robbery on December 4, 1980. The subsequent autopsy revealed that Stella Walsh possessed anatomically correct male genitalia. This surprise discovery confirmed the suspicions of some of her competitors and cast doubts on the legitimacy of her medals and records.

Perhaps after all, the diminutive Canadian sprinter who came in second place in at the 1932 Olympics actually did deserve to win the gold medal. When the story finally became public and Strike was asked if she would file a report with the International Olympic Committee (IOC), she responded with the grace and humility that made her a champion in the hearts of all Canadians.

"No, I don't think so," said Strike. "When we went out on the track that day, I accepted that field and raced against them. That was what happened that day. Eight of us ran; I came in second."

Fool on Parade

In the 1960s, most people in Canada were unaware of the serious discipline of competitive race walking. The sport has been a part of Olympic history since it was first introduced in the 1906 Olympics in Greece. Canadian Donald Linden won the silver medal in 1500-metre walk that year, but the sport has never gained the respect that it deserves because the athletes look rather funny. No one knows this more than Canadian Olympian Marcel Jobin.

Training everyday on the streets of his home in Saint-Boniface, Québec, curious bystanders would constantly stare at Jobin in his tracksuit walking in a funny way for kilometres on end down the street and wonder what could possibly be the reason this man wanted to do this to himself.

"In those days, when I went out training in my red track suit people would harass me, children would throw rocks and dogs snapped at my heels," he remembered in a Maclean's interview. "It was Québec during the 1960s, and I was the 'fool in pyjamas.'"

During his illustrious career, Marcel Jobin won the 20-kilometre Canadian championship 15 times and set close to 100 records at various distances. He was clearly the king of race walking in Canada, and he was more than proud to represent his country before a partisan crowd at the 1976 Olympics in Montréal. The man that was once ridiculed by old men and children was now recognized as an Olympic athlete and given the respect he had deserved.

Unfortunately, he came out empty handed at the 1976 Olympics and his second attempt at the 1984 Olympics yet again came up short. Although he didn't achieve international success he had succeeded in raising the profile of race walkers across the country and especially in his little corner of the world. In Saint-Boniface Québec, they no longer laughed at the "fool in pyjamas."

Canada's 100-pound Marathon Man

When you imagine the best marathon runners in the world, a picture of Billy Sherring would surely be the last thing to enter your mind. The 110-pound sliver of a man stood out in the crowd of great long-distance runners because he was so small. But despite his small stature, Canada's Billy Sherring earned his share of respect on the track.

Working as a brakeman for the Grand Trunk Railway in the Hamilton area, Billy Sherring spent every spare moment he had jogging around the city. Running was his passion, and he began his competitive career by winning several local races, including the famous Round-the-Bay Marathon (which was renamed the William Sherring Marathon after his death in 1964). Winning all those races by such decisive margins got Sherring noticed, and in 1906, he was chosen to represent Canada at the 1906 Olympics in Athens Greece. The only problem was that Sherring was left to pay for the entire trip to Athens on his own.

In the early 1900s, athletes did not have access to the same resources that most enjoy today. Many were left to their own devices if they wanted to pursue the sport on the world stage. Being a man of meagre means, Sherring could not afford to finance his trip to Athens. The community tried to rally some cash for Sherring by holding several fundraising events, but their well-intentioned efforts only managed to raise $90, clearly not enough to get him the Greece. Being of Irish descent, Sherring felt that he could count on his God-given luck to get him overseas. So he bet the entire $90 the community on a horse named Cicely...and won! Sherring arrived in Greece seven weeks before the Olympic Games and took a job at the Athens rail station in order to further finance his trip.

The course Sherring would be running was the same legendary route once traversed by the Greek soldier Pheidippides, who was sent from the city of Marathon to Athens to deliver the message that the Persian army had been defeated at the Battle of Marathon in 490 BC. As the story goes, Pheidippides ran the distance between the two cities (about 26 miles) without stopping. He burst into the Athenian senate and proclaimed, "We have won!" and then fell to floor and died from exhaustion.

The 110-pound Billy Sherring from Hamilton, Ontario, Canada would be running that same course against some of the best long distance runners in the world. On the day of the race, May 1, 1906, the temperature in Athens climbed to a blistering 100 degrees Fahrenheit, and the

Mediterranean sun afforded the runners little relief. At the start of the race, Sherring weighed in at 112-pounds. By the end, he weighed just 98 pounds—a good indication of the gruelling conditions of the Olympic marathon that day.

Initially, Sherring led the pack but by the 18th mile, he shared the lead with American runner Billy Frank. For several miles, the two runners travelled together enjoying each other's company. When Sherring felt it was time to break out on his own, he said to his American friend, "Well goodbye Billy!" and he was off.

As Sherring entered the stadium, he was met with a wave of applause from the 80,000 spectators gathered to watch the final moments of the race. For his final victory lap around the track, he was accompanied by Prince George of Greece, who ran the entire length of the track all the while emphatically applauding Sherring's triumph. A picture taken at the time shows an exhausted but exuberant Sherring near the end of his race wearing a t-shirt with a large shamrock print for good luck while a very regal Prince George in military-style dress galloping alongside politely clapping.

As Sherring entered an archway near the dressing room after the race, he was showered with roses as a triumphant hero. For that one moment, the diminutive rail man from Hamilton, Ontario, surely felt like the most important person in world. For his efforts, Sherring received a golden statue of the Greek goddess Athena and a live lamb. But not all were happy with Sherring's victory. In an extract from the magazine "Spalding Athletic Library" one writer openly lamented the Canadian's victory. "A Greek did not win the marathon race, and for the good it would have done sport, it is too bad that a runner of that nationality did not carry off the honours. To be sure, we all give credit to W.J. Sherring of Canada."

Despite the backhanded praise from these few writers, Sherring returned to his hometown as a conquering hero. The Hamilton city council, that hadn't been able to find a dime to give to Sherring to send him to Greece, suddenly came up with $5000 to hand over as a reward. The city of Toronto added another $500 to his earnings.

Sherring gave up his competitive running career after his 1906 victory in the marathon and took a desk job as a customs officer with the city of Hamilton.

The runner no one thought would win took his last step at the age of 86.

The Triumphs of Percy Williams

When Percy Williams was selected to represent Canada in the 100-metre and 200-metre events at the 1928 Olympics in Amsterdam, he quietly admitted to himself that he didn't belong among such world-class athletes. If he won anything, he felt, then the Olympics really didn't offer up much of a challenge. After easily winning his first heat in the 100-metres and then winning again in the second heat to make it into the semi-finals, Williams' extreme modesty showed in his journal entry after that day:

> *July 29, 1928: My ideals of the Olympic Games are all shot. I always imagined it was a game of heroes. Well, I'm in the semi-finals myself so it can't be so hot.*

At just 126 pounds, Percy Williams didn't seem like much of an opponent. The slender Canadian with his semi-curly hair, large nose and funny ears looked more like an accountant than your typical athlete. Even Williams knew that he wasn't the archetypical athlete you saw at the Olympic Games. But when he got on the track, he could move like lightning.

At the 100-metre sprint finals Williams was up against some imposing figures in the world of athletics all of whom towered above his 5-foot

5-inch frame. Frank Wykoff and George Lammers of Germany, Wilfred Legg of South Africa and Bob McAllister and the 200-pound Jack London of the British Isles rounded out the field of competitors.

The race began with two false starts—neither by Williams. On the third attempt, Williams was first off the line, this time without fault. The 126-pound Canadian's legs seemed to be moving at the speed of light compared with the long strides of his competitors. By the halfway point of the race, those speedy little legs had propelled Williams into a comfortable lead. With only a few metres remaining, the large Jack London began pushing his huge frame and was making ground on Williams but missed catching up on him by two steps. Percy Williams was the 100-metre Olympic Champion. He described the feeling in is journal later that evening.

July 30, 1928: Well, well, well. So, I'm supposed to be the World's 100-metre Champion. No more fun in running now.

Now began two days of gruelling running in the two hundred metres.

Now that he had shown the world what he was capable of in the 100-metre sprint, Williams wasn't entirely discounted from challenging for the gold in the 200-metres. But most still figured his small stature would be his downfall over the longer distance. Williams coach Bob Granger knew the competition like the back of his hand and had the perfect plan of action to beat the lot. His biggest challenge would be the German Helmut Koernig. The tall German had flawless running form and a precise plan when running the 200-metres, but Granger knew of one flaw in his armour.

"Koernig is your man to beat," he told Williams before the race. "He is a front runner—an inspirational runner—and if you come out of the curve even with him, or just ahead of him, you will kill his inspiration and win!"

Williams took the advice, and as they came out of the curve, he and Koernig matched each other step for step. Running neck and neck until the final few metres, Williams found that little extra bit of energy from within and drove to the finish line to win his second gold medal of the games. As happy as his coach was, he still could not figure out how Williams could pull off such dramatic upsets given his lack of style.

"I think he violated every known principle of the running game," said Granger. "He ran with his arms glued to his sides. It actually made me tired to watch him."

Percy Williams returned home to Canada a conquering hero. Everyone loves a story about an underdog overcoming the odds to win a big victory, and no one did it bigger than Percy Williams. Despite his decisive victory, there were still a few that did not believe in Williams's God-given talent, most notably the American athletics program. After setting the world record in the 100-yard dash at the inaugural British Empire Games, which were later renamed the Commonwealth Games, the Americans, who were normally among the top finishers in track and field, did not like some unknown Canadian beating all their records. Determined to show that Williams was just a one trick pony, they set a series of indoor track meets around the northern states and pitted their best runners against Williams in 21 different events. The Americans were left red in the face as Williams won 19 of the 21 events and silenced the critics once and for all. He was the greatest sprinter in the world.

Shortly afterwards, he pulled a muscle in a race and never fully recovered. He retired from running after failing to make it into the finals at the 1932 Olympics in Los Angeles. About his retirement he later said, "I was simply bewildered by it all. I didn't like running. Oh, I was so glad to get out of it all."

Jimmy Ball (1928 Olympics)

Imagine the feeling of knowing you're about to win an Olympic Gold medal. All the training and hard work comes down to that one moment when you cross that finish line and are declared the best in the world. Within two steps of the finish line, all your hard work, all the sacrifices and all the pain, are about to be exchanged for the moment of a lifetime. One step left. You look over to see the competition you left in your wake and in that moment of inattention your Olympic dreams of a gold medal are reduced to silver. This is exactly what happened to Canadian runner Jimmy Ball at the 1928 Olympics in Amsterdam, Netherlands.

With 50 metres left in the 400 metre finals, Winnipeg's Jimmy Ball could see the gold medal just a few steps in front of him. All he had to do was cross the finish line. But Ball made the classic mistake of looking over his shoulder at the end of the race rather than concentrating on finishing, and it cost him dearly. American Ray Barbuti was in second place for the entire race but began to surge ahead in the last 100 metres hoping to catch Ball at the end. When Ball looked back, Barbuti seized his chance and beat out Ball by a step. It certainly must have been a bitter pill for Ball to swallow.

Men's 4x100-metre Relay Team
1996 Barcelona

Having just come off a gold medal and world record performance in the 100-metre sprint finals, Donovan Bailey was set to lead the Canadian men 4x100-metre relay team to victory. Backed up by Glenroy Gilbert, Robert Esmie and Bruny Surin, this team was Canada's best chance at a gold medal and possibly a world record. For so long, it had been an event dominated by the Americans runners, but now for the first time, the Canadians had a group that could challenge for the top spot. To top it all off, they had world record holder and gold medallist Donovan Bailey on their side. He certainly knew how to win and come through in the clutch.

At the start of the 4x100-metre final, Robert Esmie got the Canadians off to a good start keeping the team at the front of the pack. Glenroy Gilbert took the baton next and raced a personal best down the backstretch handing it off to Canadian corner specialist Bruny Surin. By the time Surin reached Donavan Bailey, the Canadian team had taken a commanding lead. Bailey was now racing against the clock. With 15 metres left in the race Bailey glanced over his shoulder and raised his arms in triumph. Canada had won the gold medal. But, Bailey's moment of exaltation and inattention broke his stride just enough so that they missed breaking the world record by .29 of a second. The gold was fantastic, but a record would have been sublime.

Walking Controversy

Donald Linden was Canada's premiere race walker of his time. At the 1906 Olympics in Athens, Greece, the native Torontonian won the silver medal, losing out on the gold medal to American George Bonhag. The American had already competed in Athens in the 5-mile race but had been kept off the podium. Looking for another way to earn his gold medal, he turned to race walking. He had never competed in a walking race in his life let alone have any knowledge of the sport, but he figured it would be easy enough. Before the start of competition, Bonhag approached Linden for some advice on how to compete. Linden was unsure of Bonhag's motives, "So half-jocularly and half-seriously, I told him what shoes to wear, how to stride, what the rules were; and I really encouraged him to enter," said Linden in an interview with historian Henry Roxborough. To Linden's surprise on race day, he looked across the line of competitors and saw Bonhag on the other end.

But there was just one problem with Bonhag's performance in the race. Throughout the entire 1500-metre track Linden noticed that rather than executing the proper form of footwork for a race walk Bonhag half-skipped and half-ran the whole way. At the end of the 1500 metres Bonhag skipped across the line in first place with Linden just a few metres behind him in second place. Linden wasn't alone in his assessment of Bonhag's technique; two of the four judges disqualified him for improper footwork and his gold medal was taken away. But rather than let that be the end of the story, Linden did something he would later come to regret.

Wanting to show the world that Bonhag had indeed cheated and that he was the better race walker, he challenged Bonhag to a race just between the two of them to decide the real gold medal winner. The officials agreed, and the race was scheduled for the next day at 9:30 AM sharp. Linden was on the track, early as usual, and so was the Crown Prince of Greece all waiting for the arrival of Bonhag to begin the race. But Bonhag never appeared nor did he give any explanation. For some strange reason, the previous day's results were entered into the records, and Bonhag retained his gold medal while Linden was forced to swallow his pride and accept second best.

"I would have been an easy world's champion," said Linden. "But I surely talked myself out of it."

Debbie Brill: Inventor of the "Brill Bend"

Before the arrival of famed American high jumper Dick Fosbury and his patented "Fosbury Flop," high jumpers around the world leapt over the bar using what is known as the scissor kick jump. Using the scissor kick jump, it was extremely difficult for a male athlete to clear a 2-metre jump while the women could barely reach 1.75 metres.

High jumpers found the style limiting and searched for new ways to clear even greater heights. Dick Fosbury's method was to sprint diagonally towards the bar, leap off one foot leading backwards, arching over the bar then kicking out the legs to clear and then landing on the back. He began experimenting with this method in high school and used the method to win gold at the 1968 Olympics.

However when a 16-year-old Canadian from British Columbia named Debbie Brill saw this "new" style, she recognized it as her own. She had been using exactly the same technique for years although under the nickname she coined herself, "The Brill Bend."

Using her technique, Brill quickly became a force to be reckoned with on the international scene when she made her first appearance at the

1970 Commonwealth Games and took home the gold medal clearing a height of 1.78 metres. She added another gold medal at the Pan American Games in 1971. With a nice resume of international victories under her belt, Brill walked into the 1972 Olympics in Munich, Germany, as one of the favourites to finish in the top three. Although she added four centimetres to the jump that had earned her a gold medal at the 1970 Commonwealth games, it wasn't enough to crack the top three at the Munich Olympics where she finished in eighth place with a jump of 1.82 metres.

At the 1976 Olympics in Montréal, Debbie Brill had just come off a Canadian record-setting jump of 1.89 metres and was ranked 4th in the world. With the necessary experience under her belt and a partisan crowd to cheer her on, this was Brill's best shot at reaching the podium.

In the qualifying rounds Brill just could not find her stride, and after faulting a couple of times, she didn't even advance into the quarter-final rounds. Instead of calling it quits, Brill redoubled her efforts. After all, it wasn't about winning or losing. For Brill it was about longing for the pure pleasure of the perfect jump.

"I don't try to live up to what people expect of me now," she said in a television interview. "I try to do my best, and if that is enough for them then that's good."

Brill would have returned to the Olympics again in 1980 as a serious contender for a medal, but fate and politics intervened when Canada boycotted the games because of Western tensions with Communist Russia.

Amazingly enough, at the age of 31, Brill was back at the Olympics in 1984 still in competitive form. In between the 1976 and 1984 Olympics, Brill had added a silver medal at the 1978 Commonwealth Games, a bronze at the 1979 Pan American Games and another gold at the 1982 Commonwealth Games. But it was an Olympic medal that she wanted most. Although she had improved on her previous Olympic jump with a height of 1.94 metres, it was only good enough for fifth place. She would have made another return to the 1988 Olympics had it not been for a career-ending surgery to repair damaged Achilles tendons.

Debbie Brill retired from major competition, but after she recovered from her surgery, at the young age of 47, Brill won the 2000 North American Masters tournament held in Kamloops, BC with a jump of 1.65 metres. While she never won an Olympic medal, Debbie Brill was one of Canada's greatest high jumpers and the true inventor of the "Brill Bend."

The Triumph and Tragedy of Etienne Desmarteau

If you do not believe in fate and destiny, read the story of Canadian Olympian Etienne Desmarteau.

Etienne's path to the Olympics began in 1757 when his family came over from France and settled in Québec. The original patriarch of the family was a blacksmith who hung a sign outside his shop that bore the image of two crossed hammers thus earning him the nickname of Des Marteaux ("The Hammers" in English). One hundred and fifty years later Etienne Desmarteau took that family tradition into the world of athletics.

Working for the Montréal police force, Etienne Desmarteau was an incredibly strong man with an imposing physique. With a thick moustache and greased-back hair, Desmarteau looked very much like the stereotypical strongman of the day. In his youth he had excelled in football, and as he grew older and larger, athletic feats of strength became his forte. While he excelled at most athletic events, he was particularly skilled at the hammer throw.

When the 1904 St. Louis Olympics came along, Desmarteau was Canada's best hope for gold. Yet in order to compete, he had to get time off from his job with the Montréal Police department. When he asked the chief if he could get two weeks off, he said yes but told him not to expect to resume the position when he returned. Etienne took the threat seriously but could not miss the opportunity to compete in the Olympics.

Desmarteau would be competing in the 56-pound hammer throw, a weight category that dwarfs the current 16-pound hammer throw that modern athletes use. He would need all of his 6-foot 1-inch height and all his 225 pounds to throw it even 10 metres.

Desmarteau's main competition in the event would come from Irish-American John Flanagan, who had set the world record in the event just a year earlier. The Americans were working on a perfect record in the track and field event, and Desmarteau was Canada's last hope of stop the American juggernaut. The Americans had performed well in the 1904 Olympics simply because there were not many competitors from other countries at the games. The enormous distance made the cost of travel at the time high.

On the day of competition, Desmarteau walked up to the hammer throw area and wiped the sweat from his brow. Even though it was mid-September, St. Louis was suffering from an incredible heat wave. John Flanagan took one look at the burly Canadian and knew he would have to give the throw of his life to beat him.

Gripping the triangular bar attached to the weighted ball, Flanagan heaved the 56-pound weight into the air with a groan and stepped into the throwing circle. He took one deep breath, spun around once and tossed the hammer. With all the might Flanagan could muster, he threw the weight a distance of 10.16 metres.

Next up was Desmarteau. He walked into the circle and picked up the weight without so much as a whimper. The other contestants stared at each other in disbelief. With one powerful swing Desmarteau launched the weight into the air, and it landed past Flanagan's marker with a distance of 10.46 metres. Showing great sportsmanship, Flanagan and the other American competitors lifted, struggling somewhat, Desmarteau onto their shoulders and paraded him around the arena.

When Etienne Desmarteau returned home to Montréal, he was greeted at the train station as a returning hero. When it got out into the media that Desmarteau was not going to get his job back, a huge public outcry forced the police chief to reinstate Desmarteau.

Life was good for Desmarteau when he returned. He was an Olympic champion; he had his job back; and he had respect. All of what he earned was quickly wiped away, however, when he contracted typhoid fever and died just one year later. He was only 32 years old.

Olympic Track and Field Facts

- Canada has not won an Olympic medal in track and field since Donovan Bailey, Bruny Surin, Glenroy Gilbert and Robert Esmie won the gold medal in the 4x100-metre relay at the 1996 Olympics in Atlanta.

- The first Canadian to win an Olympic track and field medal was George Orton, who won a bronze in the 400-metre hurdles at the 1900 Olympic Games in Paris.

- American decathlon world record holder and gold medallist at the 1976 Olympic Games in Montréal was actually born in the game's host city while his father studied at McGill University.

- Donovan Bailey of Canada continues to hold the 1996 Olympic record he set in the 100-metre sprint, with a time of 9.84 seconds. He is the fastest Olympian in the world.

- Perdita Felicien was named after a contestant on the television game show *The Price is Right*.

- Simon Whitfield's Olympic Gold Medal was Canada's first at the 2000 Sydney Olympics.

Canada's Track and Field Record

Gold	Silver	Bronze	Total
14	15	21	50

Chapter Two

In the Pool

The Triumph and Tragedy of Victor Davis

Often named as one of the greatest swimmers Canada has ever produced, Victor Davis got his start in the lakes around his home in Guelph, Ontario. But the lakes could not hold the aspirations of this young swimmer who needed a bigger stage on which to prove he was one of the best. In competitive sports, it takes a huge amount of drive and a very strong will; Victor Davis had those in spades.

From the moment he began competitive swimming, Victor Davis was winning races. After moving his way to the top on the Canadian swimming circuit, Davis made quite the first impression on the international scene when he set a world record in the 200-metre breaststroke at the World Championships in Guayaquil, Ecuador, in 1982. He had perfect technique and the right mental attitude to win, and his competition knew they had a new force to be reckoned with on the international scene. By the time the 1984 Olympics in Los Angeles came around, Davis had already won two medals at the 1982 World Championships in Ecuador. He had added two more to that tally at the 1982 Commonwealth Games in Brisbane, Australia.

Early in 1983, Victor Davis was hit with one of the biggest setbacks of his swimming career when he contracted mononucleosis. The world record holder and world champion swimmer was forced, really for the first time in his career, to step out of the pool and take himself out of active competition. But the time off and the subsequent return to training had some positive effects on Davis' performance in the pool despite his weaknesses and initial lack of comfort in the pool. Davis' coach, Clifford Barry, spoke of that difficult return to the pool. "Victor was a world champion. It was hard work but he easily forgot how hard it was," he said." I think he needed an obstacle, to go through or go over, he needed a challenge and I think that was it."

The illness forced Davis to change his entire training routine, but he had difficulties adapting to the new approach. He had been used to hard training sessions but was now forced, for the first time in his life, to listen to his body so as not to overexert himself. But eventually Davis was back to the gruelling training regiments and on track for a spot at the 1984 Olympic Games in Los Angeles.

At the 1984 Summer Olympic Games in Los Angeles, Victor Davis was Canada's best hope for medals in the pool. After stunning the world with his performances in lesser international competitions in previous years, Davis was ready to prove to the world that he was the best in the water.

Before the start of the 1984 Olympics, Davis was interviewed by the CBC and spoke about his attitudes when it came to competing. "I think it's all within yourself, with whatever you want, whatever satisfies you. Personally being second or third doesn't satisfy me. I think I have to be the 'victor' or I'm not going to be satisfied," he said with a cool decisive tone.

Canadian swimmer Alex Baumann remembered Davis as a fierce competitor. "He was an extremely tough competitor. He would often try to psyche out his competitors. His determination, aggressiveness and consistency made him a champion," Baumann said in a January 2000 article in *SwimNews* magazine.

Davis easily made his way into the 200-metre breaststroke finals and looking across at his competitors, he knew he would have an easy time with the field. After all, he was the breaststroke record holder. However, the competition was a little watered down during the 1984 Olympics since the Soviet Union and all its satellite countries boycotted the U.S. Olympics. Missing were all the East German and Russian swimmers that had for so long been at the top of the world. But Davis was unfazed by the controversies and focused on his race.

When the starter pistol sounded the start of the 200-metre final, Davis was out in front within the first few strokes and never looked back. The boy from Guelph, Ontario, won the gold medal in the 200-metre breaststroke. And if that wasn't enough, he established a new world record, beating out the one he had set two years earlier at the world championships. Davis was again in the medal round for the 100-metre final for the breaststroke and came in second for the silver. To top off an incredible Olympic Games, he helped the Canadian team to a surprise second place finish in the 4x100-metre medley in the finals, good enough for another silver medal. Davis was at the top of his game, and he instantly became one of Canada's favourite athletes for his incredible medal count.

For his outstanding accomplishments in an event where Canada had never really figured in the past, Davis was named as Swimming Canada's Athlete of the year, and the federal government made him a distinguished member of the Order of Canada.

Between the Los Angeles Olympic Games and the 1988 Olympic Games in Seoul, Korea, Davis just kept adding to his long list of trophies and medals. But it was on the Olympic stage that Davis loved to perform. For some reason, he seemed to relish the pressure, and at the 1988 Olympics in Seoul Korea, people expected great things from Davis.

Mark Tewksbury, a first time Olympian at the 1988 Games and Davis's teammate in the 4x100-metre medley, recognized Davis's commitment to victory from the moment they first met. "I think it's safe to say there were also personality conflicts at work. We weren't necessarily the best of friends, and we were all very different people. But we had this big challenge ahead, and we had to get along," said Tewksbury, going on to talk about the role Davis played on the team. "He was such a strong person, so focused, so intent, that you couldn't help but get caught up in his belief. He held his vision out for the rest of the team. By the end of the day, the three of us shared Victor's vision. When we arrived at the pool that night, we went in believing we could get a medal."

Davis came to the 4x100-metre medley relay determined to make his mark. In his individual races he had failed to make it to the podium. His best finish was fourth in the 100-metre breast-stroke finals, just 3/10ths of a second away from a gold medal! Putting in a good effort wasn't enough for Davis, he wanted another medal around his neck and the 4x100-metre medley was his last chance.

Davis would be racing with Olympic rookie Mark Tewksbury, Sandy Goss and Tom Ponting in the race, but he made it clear from the start just who exactly was the leader on the team.

Immediately before the race, Davis acted more like a coach than as a teammate. As the teams entered into the competition area, he noticed that the rookie Tewksbury's attention was focused on all the great swimmers from the different coun-tries and not on the race ahead. Victor knew that the rookie was trapped in awe of the some of the greatest swimmers in the world, and he knew that he had to snap the kid out of his stupor. Davis literally grabbed Tewksbury's head and pulled him back into the Canadian group.

"When I looked away again, Victor grabbed my ear, stared me down and said, 'You can look at those other guys all you want, but you have to swim the backstroke leg of this relay, and if you don't swim well, I will kill you!'" said Tewksbury looking back on race day.

Up first on the platform was Tewksbury. With Davis words running through his head, Tewksbury posted a faster time than he had in his individual event, but it was only good enough to put the Canadian team in third place behind the Americans and the Russians. They still had a lot of ground to make up if they wanted to win the gold.

Davis was next in the pool to swim the breaststroke. The second-place Russian swimmer was just ahead of him in the next lane and was swimming fast. But Davis was equal to the task and narrowed the distance enough to give his teammates a fighting chance.

"After the turn, the Russian began to fade. Victor kept doing the same thing, which was this strong, steady pace. And he almost caught him—at the time, it was the fastest split ever recorded in relay. Suddenly we found ourselves fighting for silver," said Tewksbury looking back on the day.

It was up to Ponting and Goss to maintain the distance that Davis regained for the team. Two of the best Russian swimmers were left, and they were not about to give up any distance to the upstart Canadians.

Ponting kept the Canadians neck and neck with the other Russian swimmer who had in the last 12 years never lost a race in the butterfly. As Ponting huffed and puffed his way through the last few metres, he could just hear Victor screaming on the deck at the top of his lungs not to give up. When Goss jumped into the pool for the last leg, Davis could almost be heard above the screams of the crowd. Somehow Goss manage a last push at the end of the race and beat out the Russian for a second place finish and a silver medal. The Americans easily won the gold medal.

After the Olympics, Davis decided that he would retire from amateur competitions and pursue a different career path. He opened a swimming pool safety company and placement service for lifeguards. Looking to get the past few years of training and competition off his mind after his retirement, Davis relaxed like any other person his age by hitting a few bars and clubs. But on the night of November 11, 1989, Davis' peaceful retirement turned into a nightmare.

After leaving a club in the Montréal suburb of Sainte-Anne-de-Bellevue, Victor Davis was struck by a car whose driver subsequently fled the scene. Davis died just two days later from massive brain trauma at the age of 25.

Apparently, Davis had gotten into a heated argument with three men inside the bar, and when Davis, his girlfriend and another friend left the bar, the three men followed and continued their verbal assaults. Davis's girlfriend and his other friend waited in their car, and after Davis had chased the three men away, he walked across the street to get some orange juice. As he was walking back across the street, the three men returned to the scene in their car and drove straight at Davis knocking him more than 30 feet. He landed head first on a parked car. Due to lack of evidence and the Montréal police department's mishandling of the car that hit Davis, no charges were ever laid.

On January 13, 2008, the CBC ran a two-hour movie on the life and death of the Canadian champion written by and starring swimmer Mark Lutz.

The Synchronized Swimmer
with a Heart of Gold

In the world of Olympic level sports sometimes the emotional toll placed on the athlete is far greater than the physical levy they must endure. The history of the Olympics is littered with stories of athletes fighting against all odds to make their individual dreams of world glory come true. Not all have happy endings, but many are as compelling as some of the greatest dramas. Canada's Sylvie Fréchette added her story to the list when she competed in the individual synchronized swimming event at the 1992 Olympics in beautiful Barcelona, Spain.

Throughout her life Sylvie Fréchette overcame many obstacles. Born in Montréal during the summer of love in June 1967, just three years later she experienced the first tragedy in her life when her father died. Raised by her mother, Fréchette learned to be emotionally tough, but one doesn't easily overcome the loss of a parent at such a tender age. To occupy her mind, she took up synchronized swimming at the age of eight and by her teenage years was winning competitions across the country. By her mid-20s she was ready for international competition. In 1991, she burst onto the world stage, winning the gold medal in the solo event at the synchronized swimming world championship. But Barcelona was where Fréchette wanted to make her mark.

She trained tirelessly for weeks on end before the start of the Olympics to ensure that nothing could keep her from putting on her best performance. But in the months leading up to the games, it would be her personal life that would stand between her and her dreams of Olympic glory. A few months before leaving for Europe Sylvie had to deal with the death of her grandfather. It was a trying time for Fréchette , but she knew her grandfather would have wanted her to go to the Olympics and do him proud. With a renewed sense of purpose, she jumped back into her training and had an even better reason to succeed at the games. She counted herself lucky that she had great family support and the love of her devoted boyfriend and fiancé Sylvain Lake to see her through those difficult times. But with less than one week to go before getting on a plane for Barcelona, tragedy struck again.

On July 18, 1992, shortly after 3 PM Fréchette returned home from a day of training to the townhouse she shared with her fiancé. As she opened the front door, she was assaulted by the smell of exhaust fumes. All of the windows were shut, which was strange given that it was the middle of summer in humid Montréal. Searching the house she found that her fiancé had left his car running in the garage. The idea that something might be wrong suddenly flashed through her head, and she ran up to the bedroom to look for her fiancé. To her horror she found him lying dead on their bed. He had committed suicide.

Fréchette later reflected on that day in an interview with *Sports Illustrated*'s Michael Farber. "I'm alive, I'm happy, but the hole in your life never fills," Fréchette said. "I did feel guilty for a while. I doubted myself. Should I have known?" To this day Fréchette still does not know why Lake killed himself.

Miraculously, after all that she had been through, Fréchette was able to gather herself together enough to pack her bags and get on a plane for Barcelona. After a brief press conference upon arrival in Barcelona, Fréchette retreated to the quiet and safety of the Olympic village. "My body was in Barcelona, but my mind was somewhere else," she said. "I felt like I was eavesdropping on someone else's life. I was like this little robot. Little flashes come back to me. I don't remember the [Olympic] Village. The only thing I remember about the opening ceremonies is it was long and I was sitting on the wet ground at the stadium."

Thousands of cards began to pour in from all over the world. The shy, unassuming girl from Québec had won the hearts of millions of people. But mixed in with the warm wishes were harsh criticisms from a few who asked how she could have not seen the signs that her fiancé wanted to kill himself. How could she be so self-centred as to fly off to the Olympics after the love of her life died? Luckily her coach intercepted those messages, but Sylvie still had those same questions running through her mind.

With a huge weight on her chest, she managed to rally enough courage to compete in the synchronized swimming solo event. All of Canada watched with baited breath as their athlete, wearing her heart on her sleeve, jumped into the pool for her opening routine. With a brave smile across her face, Fréchette put on the best performance of her career and received a sonorous round of applause from the thousands of spectators gathered at the Olympic pool. Everyone in the building knew that Fréchette had put on a near flawless performance, but when the scores appeared on screen, one judge's assessment did not reflect the sentiment of the crowd. Among the scores ranging from 9.2 to 9.6, the Brazilian judge Maria da Silveira Lobo had given Sylvie a low score of 8.7. This low score put Fréchette in second place behind American swimmer Kristen

Babb-Sprague, just far enough out that she would not be able to challenge for first. The only problem was that the Lobo meant to give her a 9.7 and not an 8.7. Her finger had simply slipped on the key, and when in a panic she tried to correct her mistake, she pressed the wrong button and confirmed the score. Lobo tried to alert the assistant referee of her error, but the Japanese referee did not understand her pleas.

The Canadian Olympic committee made an official complaint to swimming's governing body, but their complaints fell on deaf ears. The next day Fréchette competed in the synchronized swimming final but was too far behind the American to win gold and had to settle for silver. With grace and humility far beyond her years, Fréchette accepted her medal and returned home to piece together her life.

"I was going to live my life to the full—'Watch me go' became my motto," wrote Fréchette in the book *Heroes in Our Midst*. "It lasted for a year, and then I crashed. The body is the most beautiful machine in the world but you have to look after it."

That would have been the end of the story had it not been for fellow Montréaler and former Olympic swimmer Dick Pound.

A member of the International Olympic Committee (IOC), Dick Pound had considerable pull with both the swimming governing body, FINA, and then-IOC president Juan Antonio Samaranch. He managed to persuade them to give her the medal she had originally deserved. In December 1993, before a crowd of 2000 cheering fans, Sylvie Fréchette received the gold medal she had long dreamed about.

"Maybe the ending to my story was perfect," Fréchette later explained, "but the part before was a nightmare."

Fréchette competed in one more Olympic Games, taking home a silver medal in the synchronized team event during the 1996 Olympic Games in Atlanta.

Carolyn Waldo's Story

At just the tender age of 19, Carolyn Waldo began her Olympic odyssey by competing in the solo synchronized swimming event at the 1984 Games in Los Angeles, California. The discipline of synchronized swimming might look easy due to the graceful dance of the athletes, but the sport combines artistry, endurance and strength. All of these demands combine to make the task of the perfect routine almost impossible.

Born in Montréal, Waldo's first experience with the Olympics was a memorable one. When most young athletes Waldo's age first break into the Olympics, they must consider themselves lucky just to be there. Most "first-timers" don't get to walk away with medals around their necks. Waldo's first Olympic experience was different, however. In the solo synchronized swimming event, the Canadian youngster surprised all her competitors by winning the silver medal and only just missing the gold by a few points.

She lost, but it wasn't the end of the world. "It's good for me (to lose)," she said. "I am for sure not going to throw in the towel. I know I didn't swim my best." Waldo knew that in the world of competitive sports there was always another chance at redemption.

By 1986, Waldo was one of the best in the world, and she had proven it at the World Aquatic Championship, winning three gold medals in the process. But at the height of her sport, Waldo began to doubt her future. "People expect Carolyn Waldo to walk on water, and obviously that's not possible," she said in a 1988 CBC Radio interview. "I guess I figured out where I am supposed to go from here and then I started to think of my life outside of the pool, like what else can I do but synchronize swim and it really started to worry me that I wouldn't be able to do anything else on this planet. So I basically just kick myself in the butt and said, 'Get to the pool.'"

At 23 years of age, Waldo returned to the Olympics with the experience she needed to soar to new heights.

Training in Calgary months before the 1988 Games in Seoul, Korea, Waldo and her swimming partner Michelle Cameron got to witness the excitement of the 1988 Winter Games being held that year in the city. They watched the fresh-faced excitement of the athletes running about the city. Questions, doubts, fear and joy were written into every line in their faces. They wanted to share that experience and couldn't wait to get to Seoul to begin their Olympic journey.

Arriving in Seoul months before the games started, Waldo and Cameron were able to get an initial taste of the upcoming Games. There for a pre-Olympic meet against some of the other women they would be competing against, the pair got to work on their routines in the very environment where they would soon be pushing for a gold medal. Winning the pre-Olympic meet gave them a boost, but they saw the performances of the other women, and they knew that they would have to put in a flawless performance if they wanted to take home the gold. Waldo had already missed out on the gold from the 1984 Games and did not want to experience that again. She expected the best from herself.

Waldo put all her worries aside for the opening ceremonies of the games. She was given the honour of carrying the Maple Leaf in front of the entire Canadian team. It was one of her proudest moments, but her Olympics were just getting started.

Pressure to win began to mount on Waldo and her partner after the Ben Johnson scandal deflated Canadians hopes of Olympic gold. Everyone looked to them as the favourite in their event and expected the pair to return with nothing less than the gold. Before the start of the duet finals, Waldo competed in her solo event. She clearly dominated the pack of athletes putting in a flawless and tasteful routine. Her gold medal took immense pressure off her partner's shoulders and had given Canadians the gold medal that they were hoping for.

In the pair's final, the two Canadians were up against their American rivals the Josephson twins. The twins went into the pool first for their final routine before the medals were to be handed out. The "J's" as Waldo and Cameron called them, put in a near flawless routine, scoring four perfect 10s out of seven judges. After watching a few more pairs finish their routines, it came down to the Canadians and the Americans who were vying for that top spot. Waldo and Cameron knew they would have to be perfect.

Before jumping in the pool, the pair jumped up and down to relax their muscles. Cameron took a quick look into the crowd, and it seemed to her that all of the Koreans were carrying Canadian Flags. Waldo and Cameron were attempting one of their most difficult routines: over 70 percent of the time was spent under the water! If they could pull it off, they would win the gold! After what seemed like an eternity, the pair surfaced with one final flurry, the music stopped, and the crowd began to cheer. They left the safety of the pool and waited for the judges' scores.

"I didn't really watch the marks coming up," said Cameron. "I just looked at the part of the scoreboard that showed our placing. It was a great feeling to see first place coming up. We were the Olympic Champions."

This was Carolyn Waldo's second gold medal of the games making her the first female Canadian to win two gold medals at one Olympic Games.

After the Seoul Olympics, Waldo retired from the world of competitive swimming.

Olympic Swimming and Diving Facts

- Alexandre Despatie won silver in Athens and became the first Canadian male to win an Olympic diving medal.

- At the 1976 Olympics in Montréal, Canada won a medal on the first day of competition. The women's 4x100-metre medley relay swim team of Wendy Hogg, Robin Corsiglia, Susan Sloan and Ann Jardin took home the bronze.

- Diver Ann Montminy had been to two Olympics before the 2000 Games in Sydney, Australia, but had never won a medal. Sydney was her last chance at redemption. She realized her dream when she won a bronze in the 10-metre platform event and a silver in the 10-metre synchronized diving event with Emilie Heymans. She was the only Canadian at the Sydney Games to win more than one medal.

- For the first time in decades the Canadian swimming team did not win a single medal at the 2004 Games in Sydney.

- At the 1984 Olympics, the women's springboard event was expected to be a battle for gold between the Americans and the Chinese, but Canada's own Sylvie Bernier stole the show and won gold. Finishing her dive before the final competitors Bernier had to watch in agony as one by one each diver tried to better her score with a perfect dive. But one by one, they failed to score the necessary points, and Bernier walked away with one of Canada's 10 gold medals at the 1984 Los Angeles Games.

Chapter Three

In the Ring

Lennox Lewis beats the odds

With a heavy British accent and a reputation as one of the world greatest ever boxers, it might surprise a few people to find out that Lennox Lewis fought for Canada at the 1984 and 1988 Olympics. But even though Lewis was born in London, England, he grew up in Canada and learned everything he knew about boxing around his home in Kitchener, Ontario.

With his impressive heft and long reach, Lewis was a natural boxer. But as a young man, he excelled at many other sports including football, basketball and soccer. It was under Coach Arnie Boehm that Lewis discovered the true art of boxing. Boehm quickly became a close friend and father figure to Lewis as he helped coach him to an incredible amateur record of 85 wins and 9 losses. Fifty-two of those wins were by stoppage.

With his impressive amateur record and a gold medal victory at the 1983 World Junior Championships, Lewis was selected to represent Canada at the 1984 Olympics in Los Angeles. The young Lewis looked overwhelmed facing the more experienced fighters from around the world and was eliminated in the preliminary rounds without making much of an impression. This early exit spurred Lewis to train harder, and one day, maybe to return to the Olympics.

The wiry kid from the 1984 Olympics grew into a muscular man by the time the 1988 Seoul games rolled around. During those four years, Lewis trained heavily and earned himself a reputation for a killer jab, a devastating right hand and an iron chin. But this time around, the competition was much more challenging because the eastern bloc athletes who had boycotted the 1984 Games returned. Fighting in the super heavyweight group, Lewis needed to be on his game and in perfect shape to make it beyond the preliminary rounds. Lewis knew he would have to face many roadblocks on his route to the gold medal, but he never thought that he would encounter one before the opening ceremonies.

In June 1988, Lewis was fighting against an American opponent just before the start of the 1988 Olympics and broke his thumb on the guy's face while delivering the knockout punch. This kind of injury would normally have been the end of his Olympic journey, but he took the setback as just another hurdle to jump over.

"It was actually a blessing in disguise," said Lewis. "It made me use my left jab more than before. I now use my left hand most of the time and the right for finishing off."

The broken hand and the need to adapt to a new fighting style did not seem to bother Lewis as he moved his way through the preliminary rounds of the Super Heavyweight class. Seeing Lewis box his way through the world's top amateur fighters, it became clear to many sports pundits that the skinny kid from the 1984 Olympics had returned to prove himself a contender. After dispensing with a few more opponents, Lewis made his way into the finals to face America's hope for gold, Riddick Bowe.

Bowe was a powerful opponent who possessed an annoying jab and a devastating right hand closer. This would be the biggest fight of Lewis's career.

When the bell rang for the start of the first round Lewis didn't really have a plan of attack in mind and just hoped to learn Bowe's weaknesses early on. But trying to match Bowe's inside strategy did not work in that first round. Bowe landed a few good punches that knocked the sweat off Lewis's face. Returning to his corner at the end of the first, Lewis received an earful from his coach Adrian Teodorescu for not using the left-hand jab and the right-hand bomb that had served him so well in the preliminary rounds.

Taking his coach's advice, Lewis returned determined to turn the fight around in his favour. The coach's strategy worked. He landed a series of blows and Bowe received a standing eight count from the referee. When the fight resumed, Lewis continued his attack on Bowe and landed a flurry of blows that forced the referee into another standing count. But this time, rather than resume the fight, the referee decided that Bowe had received enough punishment and stopped the bout. Lewis had overcome a broken hand to become the gold medal champion. It was Canada's first gold medal in boxing since Horace Gwynne won the top prize in the bantamweight class at the 1932 Los Angeles Olympics.

Realizing that he could make a career in professional boxing after his 1988 gold medal, Lewis returned to the land of his birth. Canada was a good place to train and gain experience, but if Lewis wanted to gain a larger profile, he would need a market capable of supporting professional boxing. Canada was good for a hockey player but not for a professional boxer. As a professional, Lewis became the undisputed heavyweight champion of the world and is known as one of the best boxers to ever step in the ring. As he moved on to greater things, he could have forgotten about his time in Canada, but he didn't, exclaiming to an HBO reporter after one of his victories, "Big up to my homies in Kitchener!"

The Long and Winding Road to Sydney

Daniel Igali grew up wrestling. Born in Nigeria, wrestling was as big a part of his culture as hockey is to Canadians. From the moment he could walk, Daniel Igali knew how to force an opponent to submit. And living in an extended family of 21 children, Igali had plenty of bodies to practice on while growing up!

Igali discovered his path in life when, at the age of 10, the Nigerian Olympic wrestler Appah Macauley, visited Daniel's village after just returning from the 1984 Olympics in Los Angeles. The stories he told of meeting people from all around the world captured Igali's attention. But it was the simple act of getting on a plane that made Igali want to be an Olympic wrestler.

Wrestling his brothers and sisters was one thing, but as he grew bigger and stronger, he realized that it just wasn't enough. Igali entered competitive wrestling in 1990, and in 1993, he became the African Champion. Having the title of African Champion was nice, but in Nigeria, there was just no money to help fund his sport. In 1992, Daniel was all set to depart for Senegal to compete in the Olympic qualification rounds, but he was turned away at the last minute for a lack of funds. To take his career to a new level, he knew he would have to make a drastic change in his life.

Everything changed for Igali when he came to Canada for the 1994 Commonwealth Games. While he placed a disappointing 11th overall, he saw a life-changing opportunity in the country. Back in his homeland, the political situation was extremely volatile, and if things got any worse, there would be no way that he could pursue his studies and wrestle at the same time. Although the decision was a difficult one, he realized it was necessary for him to move to Canada.

"It was the most difficult decision I ever had to make," he said. "My family back home was extremely upset, and so was I, but there were many people in Canada who befriended me and made it easier."

The road to the Olympics was still far off. He had to work as a dishwasher, a berry picker, a construction worker and a security guard doing graveyard shifts to pay his bills. It was difficult at first, but Igali knew he was working toward his goals and that he had come a long way already for a kid from the "fresh water swamps of Bayelsa State, Nigeria."

After some embarrassing and tough losses on the mat, Daniel Igali started making a name for himself at the World Championships in 1998. There he came in fourth place at the World Championship in Tehran, Iran. Just one year later, he won six straight bouts in the men's 65-kilogram division at the World Championship at Ankara, Turkey, to become Canada's first men's world wrestling champion. Supporting him this whole time was his adoptive host mother Maureen Matheny. She had opened up her home and her heart to Daniel and had been one his biggest sources of inspiration. But just five days after winning the World Championship, Maureen succumbed to the cancer she had been battling for a long time. It was a tragic loss for Igali because they had been so close, but it also gave him inspiration when fighting for his ultimate goal, Olympic Gold.

Now as a World Champion, it went without saying that he would qualify for the Olympics. After all his hard work, Daniel Igali finally saw his dream come to life. Nine days after the opening ceremonies, Igali stepped onto a wrestling mat in Sydney, Australia, representing his adopted country of Canada.

His first match woke him up to the realities of the high stakes competition in which he was involved. Igali barely squeaked by against his Iranian opponent and in his second match, he beat out his Cuban aggressor in another close victory that went into overtime. Igali knew he had been lucky against his first two opponents, but luck wasn't going to get him the gold. In the semi-final round against the American Lincoln McIlravy, he would have to be perfect.

The two wrestlers had faced each other five times in the past with McIlravy winning three of the five. The last time they faced off against each other at the 1999 World Championships, Igali had taken him out, but this was the Olympics. A lot more was at stake. McIlravy put in a good match, but Igali gave few openings for the American to exploit. The two titans took the match into overtime, but in the end, Igali came out the victor. After the match, McIlravy approached Igali in the dressing room and gave him a few words of support for his next match. "You are the best athlete I have ever wrestled against. Good luck. Win the Gold."

In the final round, he was up against a tough and skilled Russian opponent. Russia had a history of producing some of the best wrestlers in Olympic history, and Igali knew that the gold medal would only come if he wrestled the match of his life.

When the whistle blew, the two wrestlers locked shoulders and looked for the opening takedown. Igali played a defensive game at first, but he went on the attack at selected moments taking advantage of the Russian's few weak spots. After giving up a few points, Igali turned the match around with several quick takedowns, and when the final whistle blew, Igali had won the gold medal. By the look on his face, he could hardly believe what he had accomplished. After congratulating the Russian wrestler on a well-fought match, Igali retrieved a Canadian flag, placed it at the centre of the ring and did a celebratory jog around the Maple Leaf before bowing to kiss the flag.

When he climbed to the top of the podium to receive his Olympic gold medal, he could not stop the tears of joy from running down his face, and as that Canadian National Anthem blared over the loud speakers, he felt proud to have won the gold for his adopted country and for all those that had helped him along the way.

Today Igali continues to be an active wrestler but divides his time between speaking to kids around the country about his story and working with foundation that set up the Maureen Matheny School in his home village in Nigeria. Daniel Igali had truly come full circle.

Judo Master Nicholas Gill

When Montréal resident Nicholas Gill won an Olympic bronze medal at the 1992 Olympic Games in Barcelona, Spain, not one Canadian journalist was present to report on his achievement. He didn't care. He was happy to have a medal around his neck and something to show his friends back home.

After his bronze medal victory, Gill continued winning competitions around the world, adding a silver medal at the 1993 World Championships, two more bronze medals at the 1995 and 1999 World Championships and two gold medals at the 1995 and 1999 Pan American Games. With an impressive resume of international success, Gill walked into the 2000 Olympics in Sydney, Australia, as one of the favourites to go home with a gold medal.

There was just one fighter that Gill was hoping he would not have to face: the heavily favoured, 2000 World Champion, Japan's Kosei Inoue. Inoue had won every one of their previous four matches.

With the precision of a master fighter Gill made his way through the preliminary rounds, the quarterfinals and the semi-finals. In the final gold medal match-up, he would fight against none other than Kosei Inoue. To beat Inoue, Gill knew he would have to have the fight of his life.

The two judo masters seemed perfectly matched throughout most of the bout. But then Gill made one fatal mistake.

"I felt until the last moment, the match was going like I had planned," Gill said. "He just caught me in one of my attacks and countered me." The speed with which the match ended left Gill searching for answers and yearning for another shot at the Olympics.

The 22-year old Inoue won the bout with a textbook throw for one point—or Ippon— halfway through the five-minute bout. He raised his hands in triumph while Gill lay on the mat dejected at having lost his chance at gold. He knew the road back to an Olympic final would be paved with a lot of pain and sacrifice. Although he was proud of his silver medal, he would always be haunted at losing out in the final. He knew if he could just have one more chance at the gold he could put his mind to rest. Unfortunately, in 2003, he was almost forced to retire from competition altogether.

While competing at the Moscow Judo Grand Prix, the 31-year-old Gill was in a difficult semi-final match when he tore the ligaments in his right knee. The injury, which normally has a re-covery period of about six months, threatened Gill's chances of making it to the 2004 Olympics in Athens, Greece.

"I use my right leg very much, and I need a good knee to fight again and return to a cer-tain level," said Gill in a CBC interview. "I will go through the operation, and then I'll see how things go. I have yet to look at the situation with the Olympics. In a way it's sad to be stuck with this at this time but what can I say, when you do high performance sport, you're always vulnerable to that kind of situation. It's part of the game."

Gill underwent the knee surgery to repair the torn ligaments and began the lengthy process of rehabilitation and training to get back in shape in time for the opening of the 2004 Olympics. After a lot of pain and sweat, Gill was finally back in shape for the Olympics and was ready to proudly represent his country at the Games. He received the added honour of having been cho-sen to carry the Maple Leaf at the opening cere-monies. All seemed to go according to plan. Then a media report surfaced that Gill had voted for Québec independence during the 1995 referen-dum, putting into question whether someone who had supported the separatist movement should have been chosen to carry the nation's flag. Gill shrugged off the controversy saying that the referendum was in the past and that he was very proud to carry the Canadian flag. "To carry the Olympic flag will be my best memory from my Olympic career. It's an incredible honour."

Going into the first round of matches, Gill felt relaxed and the most at ease he had been in his Olympic career. Gone were those annoying butterflies in his stomach he had as a 20-year-old when he first faced off against some of the greatest judo masters in the world back in the 1992 Olympics. Now at the age of 32, all those worries and fears seemed silly to him.

Gill was matched up against Italian Michele Monti in the light heavyweight division for his first match-up. Everything seemed to be going right for Gill when he shot in tight for an attack, which Monti anticipated and countered by throwing him to the mat. In the blink of an eye, the match was over, and Gill's hopes of making it back to the podium were severely in doubt. He had to sit on the sidelines for nearly an hour to see if he would qualify for the remaining wild card spot, but those hopes too were dashed. Gill's Olympic dream had ended rather abruptly.

"I felt too relaxed for some reason," Gill said. "I've been feeling very good at training. Maybe that was the problem. Maybe I should have been a bit more worried."

He knew in his heart that this had been his last chance at Olympic gold. "Really now I think that will be the last one," Gill said afterwards.

Gill continued competing after the Olympics but he never realized his dream of Olympic Gold. Despite his Olympic defeat in Athens, Gill goes down in the history books as Canada's most decorated judo Olympian.

The Jockey Boxer

Although not much of a fighter when you look at him, Horace "Lefty" Gwynne had lightning quick reflexes and a deceptively powerful punch. Boxing wasn't, however, his chosen sport. Instead, the diminutive athlete made a living by riding horses whenever he could. That said, he truly loved boxing.

At just 116 pounds and no taller than 5-feet 2-inches, Gwynne didn't seem made for fighting, but once in the ring, he fought like a cornered animal with rabies. Although he had only fought in 15 matches prior to the Canadian championships, he easily won the tournament and the right to represent Canada at the 1932 Olympics in Los Angeles, California.

Most fighters like to know who they're going up against before they step in the ring, but Gwynne felt that gave the other guy the advantage. He preferred to be surprised when he got to each new round of the Olympic competition. Fighting in the bantamweight division, "Lefty" Gwynne easily handled his first round opponent from Italy, Vito Melis and won the match on points. Hi second round Philippine opponent Jose Villaneuva suffered the same fate and was taken out on points.

One fighter stood between "Lefty" and the gold medal, German Hans Ziglarski. The German was a tough fighter who was fast on his feet. But "lefty" had hands that moved faster than the German's, and in the second round of their bout, he knocked the German out cold. After a standing count, the match was called. Gwynne had won the gold medal.

When Gwynne returned home to Toronto he was welcomed as a conquering hero, and at a civic ceremony, he was given a watch from the mayor of Toronto.

After the Olympic Games, Gwynne turned professional and fought for another six years before retiring from sports. For his gold medal performance and contributions to professional Canadian boxing, he was inducted into the Canadian Sports Hall of Fame.

Olympic Boxing Facts

- Lennox Lewis wasn't the only Canadian athlete to win an Olympic medal in boxing at the 1988 Olympics. Toronto's middleweight Olympian Egerton Marcus fought his way through challengers from the Philippines, Yugoslavia, West Germany and Pakistan, before losing out in the gold medal match to West German Henry Maske. He took home the silver.

- Canada's Ray Downey completed the medal sweep, winning a bronze medal in the light middleweight division.

- At the 1984 Olympics, Toronto native Shawn O'Sullivan clearly beat American opponent Frank Tate in the gold medal final of the light middleweight class. Tate was twice given a standing eight count by the referee during the fight, but he somehow managed to come out ahead on points over O'Sullivan in the end. The crowd booed the judges mercilessly, but the decision stood. O'Sullivan had to settle for the silver consolation prize.

Chapter Four

On the Water

Silken Touch

*"The most important lessons I learned from sport
I learned rowing backwards in a wooden boat."*

—Silken Laumann

Silken Laumann's story is one of chance, tragedy, pain and ultimate redemption in a quintessential Olympic moment. After the 1992 Olympics in Barcelona, this Mississauga, Ontario' native became a hero to many Canadians and an example of an athlete's determination and strength of will in the face of insurmountable odds.

By the time the 1992 Olympics came around, Silken Laumann was already an Olympic Champion, having won a bronze medal in the Double Sculls rowing event at the 1984 Los Angeles Games with her sister Daniele. In between the Los Angeles and Barcelona Olympics, Silken added to her growing list of medals at various tournaments. She won a silver medal in the single sculls at the 1990 World Championships and a gold medal at the 1991 World Championships.

In the weeks leading up to the 1992 Olympics, Silken was favoured to finish at the top of the pack and, in training, was looking strong and smooth on the water. This is the part where tragedy enters into the story.

With just under two months before the start of the Olympics, Silken was competing in a race in Essen, Germany, and was warming up for her heat. Suddenly, the boat of the German men's coxless pair, Colin von Ettinghausen and Peter Hoeltzenbein, appeared in her line of sight and crashed directly into her boat. In a flash, she saw her Olympics dream taken away.

Silken recalled that fateful moment later, "During my warm-up, this German boat came out of nowhere. It crashed right into my right leg, severing all the muscles, tendons and ligaments from midway up my right shin all the way to the ankle."

Initial reports from the doctors were that she would never be able to walk normally. Rowing was out of the question. It was one of the worst times in her athletic career. But after a little rest and rehabilitation, her injuries began to heal faster and stronger than originally anticipated. Silken saw a ray of hope that she might still be able to make it back to the Olympics. All the doctors she saw told her to be realistic: she still had a large open wound on her leg and getting into any kind of shape to compete in the Olympics would be nearly impossible. Still, even a slight chance gave Silken reason to try harder to make it in time for the Olympics. Her journey would be painful.

To be completely ready for competition, Silken would have to undergo an intensive rehabilitation and training regime that would push her to her physical and emotional tipping point almost every day. But through the tears and moments of doubt, Silken focused on the goal ahead. Soon she realized it wasn't good enough simply to compete. She wanted to win it all.

The weeks of pain and sore muscles paid off when just five weeks after her leg was mangled, she announced to the world that she would be competing in Barcelona. The global media was simply impressed that she had made it back into competitive form, but anyone who has covered athletes would know that it is extremely difficult to come back and win after such a traumatic injury. At best, people expected her to make it through the preliminary rounds in the single sculls.

But not only did Silken make it out of the prelims, she actually powered her way into a position as one of the six finalists.

Off the line, Silken looked liked she was struggling to keep up with the leaders in the final. But she hung in steady 4th place behind the Anne Marden. Those watching on television remember the camera focusing on her boat. Physical and emotional determination was etched into every strained muscle on her face. With about 1000 metres left to paddle, the strain was clearly visible with every stroke she took. This was an athlete pouring her entire being into one single moment. The essence of sport was being defined in one athlete's determination. Somehow she discovered something within herself in that moment, pushing herself to the very limit. She edged Marden out at the finish line. Silken Laumann had achieved redemption. It wasn't gold or silver. It was bronze. But it was priceless.

In the days following her dramatic come-from-behind story, Laumann was named Canadian Athlete of the Year and was selected to carry the Maple Leaf at the closing ceremonies. She added to her Olympic medal collection again at the 1996 Olympics in Atlanta where she improved on her previous performance, taking home the silver medal in the single sculls. She lost her final race to Belarusian Ekaterina Khodovich. Silken Laumann retired from competitive rowing after Barcelona, going down as one of the greatest Canadian athletes in Olympic history.

The 1992 Rowing Team

Since rowing first became an Olympic sport, Canadians had won a few medals over the years, but never had they put in a performance like the one delivered by their contingent at the 1992 Barcelona Olympics.

In a country with more than its fair share of bodies of water Canada you might figure would be a competitor in the Olympic boating competitions. The Barcelona Games elevated Canada to a whole new level, led by the women's team.

Rowing is one of the Olympics' most demanding sports. It places a heavy workload on all the muscles in the body and requires intense mental concentration. To be successful in rowing, the athletes must be extremely dedicated to their training. At the Barcelona Games, Canada showed the world just how dedicated their athletes were.

At the top of the pack was Canadian golden pair Kathleen Heddle and Marnie McBean. The pair performed like poetry on water, but out of the boat, they were two completely different personalities. Heddle was the shy introvert who never spoke much at press conferences, keeping her words short and to the point. McBean was the spitfire of the group. She was always talking and living off the emotion of the moment. Combined, the two polar opposites balanced each other perfectly on the water.

They got the world's attention when they powered their way through the preliminary rounds of the Coxless Pairs event, putting pressure on the German and Chinese teams that were the hands-down favourites. But in the final race, Heddle and McBean were in complete synchronization. Heddle powered away to set the boats' pace. McBean ensured the boat went in a straight and smooth line. Despite their performances in the preliminaries, many still did not believe the Canadian pair could challenge for the top spot. The media barely gave them any press time. The biggest story in Canadian rowing was the comeback of Silken Laumann after her horrible accident.

But the two Canadians ignored the expectations and rowed a perfect race. Heddle set a speedy pace from the beginning, and McBean steered the boat straight and true, slicing over the surface of the water. The other teams struggled just to keep up with their blistering pace, but none managed to catch the Canadians.

Heddle and McBean powered their way over the finish line comfortably in first place. The German boat was a full second and a half behind. In third place were the Americans.

The other Canadian women's team making waves at the Banyoles, which was the site of the Olympic boating events, were Kristen Barnes, Jessica Monroe, Brenda Taylor and Kay Worthington who competed in the Coxless fours event. The young Canadians surprised the favoured U.S. team and the Germans by powering their way to the finish line with smooth and powerful rowing. They won gold!

Heddle and McBean later competed in the Women's Eights event with Kristen Barnes, Shannon Crawford, Megan Delehanty, Jessica Monroe, Brenda Taylor, Lesley Thompson and Kay Worthington. The team easily powered their way to another gold medal beating out the Romanian boat by a full four seconds.

As if three gold medals weren't enough for the Canadian team, the men's eights team composed of Darren Barber, Andrew Crosby, Mike Forgeron, Robert Marland, Terrence Paul, Derek Porter, Michael Rascher, Bruce Robertson and John Wallace managed to add to the tally. The Canadian men had a tougher time than the ladies in getting their gold medal, battling the powerful Romanian boat the entire length of the race. In fact, the race was so close in the end that the Canadian men only won by .14 seconds. Whatever the margin, the win was good for gold.

Silken Laumann, of course, capped off the Canadian team's amazing showing in these two days of rowing with her dramatic comeback victory to win a bronze medal.

For a country that had previously won only a handful of medals, four golds and a bronze in one Olympics set a record. It was Canada's best performance over any two-day period in the Summer Olympics.

Heddle and McBean Continue their Winning Ways

After proving that Canadians were now a powerful force in international rowing at the 1992 Barcelona Games, Heddle and McBean returned to the 1996 Games in Atlanta to show the world again just what Canada was made of. Surprisingly, however, the pair almost didn't make it back to the Olympics at all.

After their brilliant performance at the Barcelona Olympics, Heddle and McBean went their separate ways. Having achieved her goals in rowing, Heddle retired from amateur competition, finished her degree in psychology and got a job working for a magazine. Heddle was content with her life and was willing to put the Olympics behind her. McBean, however, wanted more. After 1992, she received corporate sponsorship from shampoo and milk companies. Competition was still in McBean's blood, and she was not willing to settle for a regular job just yet. Striking out on her own, she attempted to dethrone Silken Laumann for the Canadian National title but was unable to keep up with the veteran rower. McBean needed her partner back, and in 1994, she convinced Heddle to return to competition.

Rather than re-enter the Straight Pair competition where they had already proven to be champions, Heddle and McBean wanted to try their hand at the Double Sculls. The strategy was completely different than the straight pair event. In the straight pair each rower has only one oar while in the double sculls the rowers each have two oars. The techniques of paddling a boat change drastically when each rower controls two oars. As the stroke sculler, Heddle set the pace, while McBean adjusted to keep the boat going in a straight line, and Heddle always set a blistering pace.

In the finals at Atlanta, the Canadian's were not favoured to win the gold because the Chinese and Dutch teams had performed well in races leading up to the Olympics. But the Canadian pair had been in this position before. When the pistol sounded in the double sculls finals, Heddle and McBean led the charge. The Chinese were their biggest threat throughout the race, but the two determined Canadians pulled off a victory over the Chinese by two seconds.

"It felt as if we were moments away from having nothing left," said McBean after the race. "The crowd was going crazy and I'm thinking, 'Where's the finish line?'"

When they crossed the finish line, the two rowers collapsed in exhaustion and could barely lift their heads to salute the cheering crowd. Without realizing it, they had set a Canadian record, winning their third gold medal. No one had ever accomplished that before. They added another medal to their amazing collection when they helped fellow Canadians Laryssa Biesenthal and Diane O'Grady win the bronze medal in the quadruple sculls.

Only One in Rome

Ever since 1900 when the first Canadians competed in the Olympic Games our athletes have returned home with at least two medals to show off proudly. Except at the 1960 Olympics in Rome, Italy! There Canada had its worst showing ever, bringing home a solitary silver medal. Of the 97 athletes sent to the games only the men's eights rowing crew of Donald Arnold, Sohen Bin, Ignace D'Hondt, Nelson Kuhn, John Lecky, Lorne Loomer, William McKerlich, Archibald McKinnon and Glen Mervyn managed to win silver.

The Canadian boat put in a valiant effort against the favoured German boat. Throughout the race the two boats traded the lead. But the Germans pulled ahead in the last few hundred metres and crossed the finish just one second ahead of the Canadian boat. The Czechoslovakian boat rowed to a third place finish three seconds behind the Canadians.

A True Olympic Hero

Over the years that athletes competed at the Olympics, there are countless stories of men and women triumphing over adversity with heroic effort. But none embody the definition of a hero as much as Canadian Lawrence Lemieux.

The Canadian sailor Lemieux raced in the finn class of boats at the 1988 Olympics in Seoul, Korea. On that particular day the winds on the water at Pusan started out at an acceptable 15 knots per hour. Lemieux's race was going particularly well. He was second at the halfway point and within striking distance of the leader. But it was becoming difficult to hold his boat steady as the winds whipped up 35 knots per hour, creating very choppy waters. With a shot at gold in sight, Lemieux happened to look off to where another race was being held and noticed that one of the competing boats had overturned. Both crew were in the water struggling to overturn their boat, leaving them at risk of drowning or being carried out to sea.

In a split second, Lemieux had to decide whether to give up his dream of Olympic gold or to save the life of the two sailors. The decision was easy. Lemieux steered his boat toward the overturned Singaporean boat. One of the men's hands was cut, and he was struggling just to hold on to the capsized craft. The other bobbed up and down barely keeping his head above water. Lemieux struggled to control his boat as he moved in on the man floating free in the water. Coming up close, he grabbed him and hauled him aboard. He then positioned his boat beside the man clinging to the overturned boat and pulled him to safety as well. Falling back into the now-crowded boat and breathing an incredible sigh of relief, they waited for a patrol boat to arrive.

Once the two Singaporean sailors were safely in the patrol boat, Lemieux continued with his race, but he could not make up the distance. He finished in 21st place overall!

Though Lemieux did not win his race, at the medal ceremony, IOC President Juan Antonio Samaranch awarded him the Pierre de Coubertin Medal for Sportsmanship to honour his heroism. "By your sportsmanship, self-sacrifice and courage," said Samaranch, "you embody all that is right with the Olympic ideal."

Lawrence Lemieux retired from sailing soon after and never realized his Olympic dreams. But there are two very happy people in Singapore who give thanks every day that he did not finish his race.

Olympic Boating Facts

- It's all in the family. Both parents of Mylanie Barre were themselves Olympians. Her father competed for Canada at the 1972 and 1976, and her mother won two medals (silver and a bronze) at the 1984 Olympics in kayaking. Mylanie Barre took after her mother in kayaking but did not win a medal at the 2004 games in Athens.

Chapter Five

Canada at the Paralympic Games

The Paralympics began as a means to help disabled veterans of World War II rehabilitate physically and psychologically from the trauma of war. The Paralympics were first launched in 1948 when Sir Ludwig Guttman organized the International Wheelchair Games to coincide with the 1948 Olympics in London. The first games proved a success, but organizers noticed that by limiting the games simply to those with wheelchair disabilities, they were leaving out many others who could have competed in similar events. The Paralympics now involve athletes who are blind or partially sighted, paraplegics and quadriplegics, athletes with cerebral palsy and amputees. Since 1996, athletes with mental disability have also been given full medal status.

The Paralympic Games were added to the Olympic calendar in 1960, and athletes must meet a high standard of physical prowess in order to be eligible for competition. At the first official Paralympic Games in Rome in 1960, there were some 400 athletes competing in various events. At the last Paralympics in Athens, Greece, there were over 1300 from 130 different countries. Canada first entered the Paralympics at the 1968 Games in Tel Aviv, Israel. Canadian athletes have consistently finished at the top of the medal rankings. Our best showing was at the 1984 Paralympics when they won an incredible 200 total medals.

Superwoman Chantal Petitclerc

Chantal Petitclerc lost the use of her legs at the age of 13 when a barn door fell on her. Before then she didn't really enjoy sports. Only after the accident did she discover her true path in life with the help of her friend and then physical education teacher, Gaston Jacques.

It can happen that after someone loses the use of a part of their body in the prime of their life that they fall into a depression and often wonder why something like this has happened to them. Chantal Petitclerc's physical education teacher knew to avoid that depression and a cycle of regret, he had to involve Chantal in sports. After some convincing, Petitclerc decided to give swimming a try in order to build up her strength and stamina. It was later, while studying at the Université Laval in Québec City that she discovered wheelchair racing.

Completely unfamiliar with the sport, Petitclerc decided to give it a try. Using a homemade wheelchair, she came in dead last in an early competition but fell in love with the sport, starting a lifelong love affair with athletics.

By the late 1980s, Petitclerc was winning every national race she entered. A big dreamer, Petitclerc made the jump into international competition and began another path in her career that would elevate her to an entirely different level. Not content with just one discipline, Petitclerc now a versatile athlete, competed in everything from the 100-metre sprints to full wheelchair marathons. By 1992 she was ready to take on the world at the Paralympics in Barcelona, Spain.

She returned from those Games in Barcelona with two bronze medals and an even greater desire to prove herself. At the closing ceremonies, Petitclerc was already looking forward to the next games in Atlanta in 1996.

At the 1996 Paralympics in Atlanta, she entered five different events and took home medals in each one. With sheer power and flawless technique, she powered her way to three gold medals in the 100-metre, 200-metre and the 400-metre races and added two more silver medals in the 800-metre and the 1500-metre races. Her Paralympic prowess continued in Sydney, Australia, where she won four more medals—two silver and two gold. But now there was something greater than medals that Petitclerc was fighting for. She wanted recognition for paralympic athletes as well.

She had long argued that athletes in wheelchairs are no different than athletes that use, for example, bicycles. But there seemed to be a stigma attached to disabled people and disabled sports in general. Although the Olympic committee had made wheelchair racing a demonstration sport at several games, it had never received full recognition.

In response to Petitclerc's voice and those of hundreds of disabled athletes who stood with her, several disabled sports were given full medal status at the 2002 Commonwealth Games. Petitclerc seized this incredible opportunity, winning the gold medal in the 800-metre race. For Petitclerc, it was a dream come true.

"You've seen a dream come true tonight," Petitclerc said at a press conference after the race. "All three of these medals—gold, silver and bronze—are very meaningful. We've been a demonstration sport since 1984 at the Los Angeles Summer Olympics—and so many summer Olympics, Commonwealth and Francophone Games that have followed—and have finally received our due. It feels wonderful in more ways than one. I've really felt true recognition from the other athletes—that we are as much high-calibre athletes as they are."

As good as it felt to have a Commonwealth gold medal around her neck, she always kept her sights on winning full Olympic recognition. She remained realistic about her hopes, however. "The Olympic barriers might be harder to break."

At the age of 35, Petitclerc entered her fourth Paralympic Games. Age could not slow down this incredible athlete as she went on to collect five more medals in the 100-metre, 200-metre, 400-metre, 800-metre and the 1500-metre races—all of them gold.

Now close to 40 years old, Petitclerc closes in on another Paralympic Games. With nothing left to prove to the world, if she enters the next Games, it will be for the sheer pleasure of competition, a pleasure she has felt since she lost her first race.

Rick Hansen: Man in Motion

Involvement in sports had always been a pursuit of Rick Hansen's. Even before his paralysis at the age of 15, Hansen was heavily involved in athletics with his high school. So when he was paralyzed from the waist down after a car crash, Hansen never thought for a second about giving up the sports that he loved. He would just have to do them a little differently.

After extensive rehabilitation, Hansen recovered from his accident, graduated from high school and entered into the physical education program at the University of British Columbia. After graduating from university, still filled with boundless energy, Hansen set out on a new path in life. He wanted to become a Paralympics champion.

Since his accident Hansen had found a passion and a talent in middle- and long-distance wheelchair races, and in 1980, he made his first appearance, representing Canada at the 1980 Paralympics in Arnhem, Holland. The inspirational Canadian beat out all other competition in the 800-metre event, winning the gold medal. He just missed out on another gold in the 1500-metre race but won silver. Already the pride of many Canadians, Rick Hansen set out on another adventure that would bring him worldwide attention and make him into a Canadian sports legend.

One year after winning his final Paralympics medal, Hansen pushed his wheelchair out of Vancouver, BC and set out on a journey that would take him over more than 40,000 kilometres and through 34 different countries. Dubbed the "Man in Motion World Tour," Hansen was on a mission to raise funds and awareness about spinal cord injuries. By the time he returned to Canada to wheel across his home nation, he had raised over $26 million for research.

Today the four-time Paralympian lives in Richmond B.C. and continues to fight for the causes close to his heart.

Arnie Boldt: Olympian on One Leg

When Canadians think of our greatest disabled athletes, several greats immediately came to the forefront of our shared history. Rick Hansen, Terry Fox and, most recently, Chantal Petitclerc are just a few athletes that have made a name for themselves Canadian sports history. But few Canadians know anything about the accomplishments of Osler, Saskatchewan, native Arnie Boldt.

After, losing his right leg in a farm accident when he was just three years old, Boldt never felt the stigma that many disabled people sometimes have, because in his community, physical injury was rather commonplace. So when Boldt took an interest in track and field at a young age, no one ever suggested that a guy with one leg couldn't compete.

Through most of his athletics career Boldt competed against other disabled athletes, but he is most famous for competing against the able-bodied in high jump competitions with his University of Saskatchewan and University of Manitoba track teams. Boldt didn't make the team because of other people's pity. He was a viable athlete who could beat even the best of the able-bodied competitors! Most of his competitors would probably admit that they didn't think that

Boldt could possibly keep up the same pace as them, but once they saw Boldt's unforgettable approach and jump, they immediately changed their tune.

Since Boldt only had one leg he obviously could not take a running start on the high jump like other athletes. Boldt solution was a simply three-hop lead up to his execution of the traditional Fosbury Flop over the bar. And he was good at it!

Boldt took his amazing athletic ability to the Paralympics for the first time in 1976, competing in the high jump, the long jump and the men's volleyball team. He struck a strange figure out on the playing field, but Boldt could compete with the best Paralympic athletes in almost any event.

Boldt regularly jumped heights of 1.90 metres or higher and was in a class all his own. At the 1976 Paralympics, he won the high jump gold and added more hardware with a gold in the long jump, setting a world record for disabled athletes of 2.96 metres—a distance not many able-bodied people could achieve!

He was so good at his craft that he won gold in the high jump at the 1980, 1984, 1988 and the 1992 Paralympics, setting world records each time. His high jump record peaked at 2.01 metres. He added gold medals in the long jump in 1980 and a silver medal in 1988. He retired from active competition in 1993 as one of the most prolific Paralympic athletes in Canadian history.

Quick Paralympic Facts

- Canadian Wheelchair basketball athlete Chantal Benoit was so dominant in her sport that she was dubbed the "Michael Jordan of Wheelchair Basketball." Her amazing skills on the court helped the Canadian team win the basketball gold at the 1992, 1996 and the 2000 Paralympics.

- Blind swimmer Timothy McIssac won five Paralympic medals at the 1980 Games in Holland, four of which were in world-record time. He added to his amazing collection in 1984, winning seven more medals.

- To this day Chantal Petitclerc holds the Canadian record in the 100-metre, 200-metre, 400-metre, 800-metre and 1500-metre events.

- During the 2004 Paralympic Games, Petitclerc set three world records and one Paralympic record.

- She holds records in the 100 metres (16.33 seconds); the 400 metres (51.91 seconds); and the 1500 metres (3 minutes, 26.89 seconds)

- She also holds the Paralympic Record in the 800 metres (1minute, 50.60 seconds)

- The song "St-Elmos Fire (Man in Motion)" from the movie of the same name, was written by fellow British Columbia native David Foster to honour Hansen's incredible achievements.

Canada at the Paralympic Games – Medal Totals

Year	Location	Gold	Silver	Bronze	Total
1968	Tel Aviv, Israel	16	6	7	19
1972	Heidelberg, Germany	5	6	9	20
1976	Toronto, Canada	28	18	32	78
1980	Arnhem, Holland	71	37	27	135
1984	New York U.S.A. & Stoke-on-Trent, U.K.	80	65	55	200
1988	Seoul, Korea	53	44	52	149
1992	Barcelona, Spain	27	20	32	79
1996	Atlanta, U.S.A	24	23	24	71
2000	Sydney, Australia	38	33	25	96
2004	Athens, Greece	28	19	25	72
Totals		360	271	289	920

Chapter Six

Canadian Olympic Facts and Other Sports

And the Medal in Art Goes to....

There was a time when it wasn't just the athletes who received all the glory for their achievements in the world of sport. At one time, people thought it relevant to reward dedicated artists who venerated Olympic athletes in their works. Whether literature or painting, this art portrayed to the world the glorious victories and agonizing defeats.

From 1912 until 1948, the International Olympic Committee sought to reward the best in the world in art. From noted painters such as Giovanni Pellegrini and sculptors like Jean Rene Gaugin to writers like the Baron Pierre de Coubertin, medals of gold, silver and bronze were handed out to top artists in many categories. From 1912 to 1948, the IOC gave medals in 19 artistic categories: Applied Graphics, Architectural Design, Designs for Town Planning, Drawings and Water-Colours, Graphic Art, Literature, Literature Dramatic Works, Literature Epic Works, Lyrics, Merit for Aeronautics, Merit for Mountaineering, Paintings, Music: Composition for One Instrument, Music: Composition for Orchestra, Music: Composition for Voice, Music, Sculpture, Sculpture Medals and Sculpture Relief.

Initially many countries hesitated at the notion of an art competition because of the extremely subjective nature of the medium, but the idea eventually caught on and made its first appearance at the 1912 Olympics in Stockholm, Sweden. The initial number of entrants was disappointing: only 35 artists were known to have sent in works for the competition. Although medals were handed out, no one really took the competition seriously. It wasn't until the 1924 Olympics in Paris that the competition gained some credibility when 193 artists sent in their works for judgement.

Canada added its name to the list of Olympic art medal winners in 1932 when Robert Tait McKenzie won a bronze medal in Sculpture Relief's for his bronze work titled "Shield of the Athletes".

The only other Canadian to win an art medal was John Weinzweig, who won a silver medal in the Music: Composition for One category.

Canada Without a Flag

The 1920 Olympics in Antwerp, Belgium, are not well remembered because most of the countries were still attempting to recover from the ravages of World War I. This was a blessing for the Canadian contingent at the games as not many people noticed their blunder.

If the opening ceremonies are famous for one thing, it is the procession of athletes through the Olympic stadium standing proudly behind their nations' flags. The countries' names are called out, and out walks a single chosen athlete proudly carrying a nation's flag. Behind, an army of athletes proud to represent their country march behind that symbol. Unfortunately, in 1920, the Canadians did not have that privilege.

Vancouver Fireman Archie McDiarmid, who was at the Games representing Canada in the hammer-throw competition, was chosen to carry the country's flag. But for some unknown reason, just before Archie was about to lead his country out onto the parade grounds someone noticed that they didn't have a flag for him to carry. Ever the 1920s moustachioed gentleman, Archie simply grabbed the pole and carried it out bare for the entire world to see. The Canadians held their heads up proudly even though they could see a few ladies in stands politely giggling behind their hands and wide brimmed hats.

Archie McDiarmid came in fourth in the hammer throw that year.

Canada's Summer Ice Hockey Gold

It has gone down in the history books that Canada's first gold medal in Olympic ice hockey came at the Winter Olympics in Chamonix, France, in 1924. But technically Canada won its first ever Olympic ice hockey gold at the 1920 Summer Olympics in Belgium.

The Winnipeg Falcons had just come off an incredible season in the Senior Amateur Hockey League winning the Allan Cup Championship. After their display of superior hockey skills, they were asked by the International Olympic Committee to join their fellow Canadian athletes at the 1920 Olympics in Antwerp, Belgium. It did seem a little strange that an ice hockey team was being invited to compete in the Summer Games, but they had also invited figure skaters to the Olympics, so it appeared that the IOC was pushing to open a new winter version of the Games.

With dreams of Olympic gold in their heads, the Canadian men's hockey team bulldozed their way through the competition beating the U.S., Sweden and Czechoslovakia by a combined score of 28–1.

In addition to their shinny new medals, the Canadian hockey team received an official piece of paper stating that they had indeed won the hockey gold medal of the first official Winter Olympic Games. The Winnipeg Falcons beamed with pride at the gold medals around their necks, knowing that they would go down in history as winning in the first ever Winter Games. But years later, the IOC repealed their decision to name the 1920 Olympic Games as the first Winter Games and handed that honour to the 1924 Chamonix, France Winter Olympics.

At those 1924 Olympics, the Canadian hockey team won the gold medal and was officially given the recognition as the first team to win Olympic hockey gold. It was only until many years later that the 1920 Winnipeg Falcons were recognized as official Olympic champions...for the 1920 *Summer* Games.

The Olympic Golfer

When you picture the archetypical Olympian, images of the tall, muscular, graceful athletes competing in the Games of ancient Greece and in the stadiums of the modern Olympiad probably come to mind. Most people would never conjure up the image of someone dressed in newsboy cap, checked sweater and slacks carrying a golf bag. But one Canadian who dared to defy convention to realize his Olympic dreams—George Lyon of Toronto—fit that image to a tee.

George Lyon was unlike any other Olympian. While most athletes spend a good portion of their lives training and playing the sports that they love, golf was never Lyon's first love. Instead, he preferred to play baseball and cricket. Lyon only took up golf on a dare. But he quickly discovered—when he was 38 years old—that he was a natural.

Lyon was unlike most competitors at the Olympics. First of all he wasn't much of an athlete. He sported a rather rotund beer belly, loved to tell a good joke and had a tendency to suddenly walk on his hands for no apparent reason. His golfing technique left a lot to be desired as well. One New York critic described him as having a swing that looked like he was "using a scythe to cut wheat."

While newspapers were busy criticizing his form and technique, Lyon was busy winning tournaments. At the age of 46, Lyon wanted to try a different type of tournament and signed up in the golf event as Canada's representative at the 1904 Olympics in St. Louis, Missouri. Eight competitors began the tournament. Of them, Lyon was the only one from outside the United States. This, of course, made him a target for the partisan U.S. newspapers. But Lyon took all the heat in stride, letting his game to do the talking for him.

"Whether I play like a sailor or a coal heaver, I never said that I am proud of my form," he wrote in a letter to the United States Golf Association after receiving lengthy critiques from U.S newspapers. "I only do the best I can."

The tournament would pit two golfers against each other in a playoff-type format. They would play through preliminary rounds and semifinals. Then a final two 18-hole rounds would decide the gold medallist.

True to his character and form, Lyon breezed easily through the preliminary rounds. He had a difficult time in the semi-finals but won, moving into the finals against a boy 23 years younger than he.

Chandler Egan may have been just 23 years old, but he was no novice. He had been recently crowned American champion and would prove to be a formidable opponent for the older Lyon. Most pundits of the day put their money on the young Egan to run away with the gold. Lyon responded to the verbal slights by walking up to the tee on the first hole and smacking the ball within eight feet of the pin. While Lyon was close enough to the pin for the birdie, Egan could only manage a par. For the next 18 holes, Egan matched Lyon shot for shot but still could not manage to make up the one stroke difference. In the second round, wisdom began to pull away from youth. By the 24th hole, Lyon had a comfortable four-stroke lead. Egan tried everything he could to make up the difference. But a couple of shots in a water hazard gave Lyon the title of Olympic Golf Champion. As he sank the last ball of the day, hundreds of fans that had gathered to watch the historic game descended upon Lyon. After many pats on the back and congratulations, a path was cleared to the clubhouse where Lyon received his medal. But instead of striding triumphantly to the podium, the 46-year-old, with boundless energy, decided to walk to the podium on his hands. And the crowd loved it!

At the 1908 Olympics in London, England, golf was again placed on the event roster, and

Lyon made the long voyage across the Atlantic to defend his gold medal. But a dispute between UK golfers and IOC officials led to the British boycotting the tournament. The Americans pulled out of the tournament as well, unwilling to travel to London when officials could not even tell them if there was going to be a tournament at all. This left Lyon as the only official entry. Officials told Lyon that he would be awarded the Olympic gold medal by default, but he refused to accept on the grounds that he did not want a prize that he had not earned. Golf was never put on the Olympic calendar again.

Canadian George Seymour Lyon remains golf's first and only Olympic gold medallist!

Canada Wins Soccer Gold

It's hard to imagine a country like Canada, known more for its cold weather and ice hockey, winning a gold medal in soccer at the Olympics, but that is just what the Ontario Galt Football Club did when they played at the 1904 Olympics in St. Louis, Missouri.

There is, however, a footnote that needs to be added to their achievement. Because the games were held in St. Louis, most of the European countries decided not to attend. The 4000 miles of ocean and 1000 miles of land separating the Old World and the New was just too long a journey. This left the 3rd Olympic Games with competitors mostly from Canada and the United States.

In the soccer competition, the Galt Football Club fought for the gold medal against two teams from the U.S.—the Christian Brothers College team and the St. Rose School team, which played in a local St. Louis amateur league.

During those first few years of the Olympic Games, it was the job of athletes to get themselves to the Olympics at their own expense. If they happened to win a medal, all your home country was likely to do was give you a hearty pat on the back.

Luckily, the Galt Club managed to raise the funds necessary to travel to St. Louis to meet the two local teams. The team beat out its first opponents, the Christian Brothers, by a score of 7–0. The following day, they managed to trounce the St-Rose School by a score of 4–0. While the two American teams battled it out for the silver medal, the Canadians received their gold medals. According to the *Toronto Mail and Empire* of November 14, 1908, the medal ceremony went as follows: "Following the second game the Galt aggregation, numbering about 50 persons, retired to the office of James E. Sullivan, chief of the Department of Physical Culture where they received their prize. After a short talk by Mr. James A. Conlon, of the Physical Culture Department, Mayor Mundy of the City of Galt, presented each player on the winning team with a beautiful gold medal."

On their way back to Canada, the team stopped off in Chicago to play the Chicago All-Star soccer team and beat them by a score of 4–2. When their train finally pulled into the station back in Canada, they were welcomed by a few thousand cheering fans.

The gold medal remains Canada's only soccer medal in Olympic history.

Gymnastic Gold

Canada had never faired very well in the Olympics gymnastic competition. It was and always has been a sport dominated by the Russians, the Chinese and the Americans. They were better funded, better trained and better coached. Against those odds, Canadian gymnasts never stood a chance. Before the 2004 Games in Athens, Canadian gymnasts had only collected three medals. Lori Fung won gold in the all round rhythmic gymnastics competition at the 1984 Games at Los Angeles; and Karen Cockburn and Mathieu Turgeon both won bronze at the 2000 Games in Sydney on the trampoline. When it came to the higher profile gymnastic events, Canada was shut out. That is until Calgary, Alberta, native Kyle Shewfelt came along.

Shewfelt's long journey to the Olympics began when his older brother taught him how to cartwheel at the age of three. Just several years later, a six-year-old Shewfelt entered a local gymnastics program training at the Altadore Gymnastics Club in Calgary.

Shewfelt was a quick study and soon finished in the top 10 of most competitions he entered. In a moment of karmic fate, at the age of nine, Shewfelt was interviewed by a local news station about kids and gymnastics. When asked what he wanted to do in his life, he answered that he was going to win a gold medal.

Shewfelt's path to the Olympics began when he entered his first international competition. He won gold in the floor exercise at the Austrian Youth Invite in 1996. He continued winning medals and placing near the top of all the competitions he entered, earning him a spot on the Canadian Olympic team at the 2000 Games in Sydney, Australia.

Shewfelt was just 18 years old then and not expected to place high in his events, but he finished in a respectable 12th place in the floor exercise and 26th in the vault. But for Shewfelt, the Sydney Olympics were less about winning a medal than about gaining the experience and confidence he needed when he returned in 2004.

Shewfelt vaulted his way up in the international rankings just before the Olympics when he finished the 2003 World Championships in Anaheim with bronze medals in both the floor exercise and the vault. The accolades that began to pour in were great, but Shewfelt was already looking towards Athens.

Having qualified for the 2004 Olympic Games, Shewfelt left his parents' home and boarded a plane heading to the place where the Olympics were born. Newspapers and magazines were all placing Shewfelt in the top three athletes expected to walk away with medals. Stories like that are hard to ignore, but he had to in order to concentrate on his objective.

In the early competition, Shewfelt tumbled and jumped his way into the top tier and was finally battling for the gold medal with Romanian Marian Dragulescu.

It came down to one final floor routine. The announcer called out "Kyle Shewfelt, Canada," and he walked into the corner of the mat. Before he even took a single step, he heard someone in the crowd yell out, "We love you Kyle!" With that he began his routine. Shewfelt was flawless in his execution, and on the final round of flips and vaults, he stuck his final landing. He earned a score of 9.787, good enough for the gold medal. Back in his hometown of Calgary, his family watched nervously as he tumbled through the air and cheered when he won. All that is but his grandmother. "I'm totally excited but not that surprised—I was expecting it," 74-year-old Trude Tackaberry said after her grandson won Olympic gold. She had seen gold in his future when he was just six. "All the kids were athletic...when Kyle got to about six they put him in hockey, and right away he could skate," she said. "He was a natural."

The victory gave Canada its first-ever Olympic gold in artistic gymnastics and its first of the Athens Olympics. Head judge for the floor exercise Hardy Fink had nothing but positive things to say about the Canadian's performance, describing Shewfelt's tumbling routine as "the best that's ever been. There is a virtuosity to his performance that even a layman can appreciate."

Shewfelt was hoping to follow up his outstanding performance with another medal in the vaulting competition, but he ended up finishing in fourth place amid some controversy. Some felt that the third place finisher, Romanian Marian Dragulescu, did not deserve the bronze because of a fall on his second vault. Shewfelt's performance was not perfect, but to everyone in attendance—except for the judges—it was apparent that he deserved the bronze and not the Romanian. Suspicions were further inflamed when it was discovered that leader of the Olympics technical committee was also a Romanian. The Canadian Olympic Committee filed a formal complaint but later dropped their request when the process stalled. Another medal would have been nice, but Shewfelt still had a gold around his neck.

"It's my second Olympics, and I credit my 2000 Olympics to my success (in Athens). I learned what the Games are like, the experience, the excitement," said Shewfelt after winning gold. "The night before, I was trying to sleep, but I was going through my routine in my head. I wasn't too nervous, but I was trying to make it perfect. The next morning, when I got up, I went into the bathroom, and I'm sort of scratching my head, and I looked at myself in the mirror, and I thought 'I look like an Olympic champion today.'"

Since that fateful day, Shewfelt's life has changed drastically; he no longer lives with his parents, and he has raised the profile of gymnastics in Canada.

Recently, his hopes for repeating as Olympic Champion in the Beijing Olympics in 2008 were seriously put at risk when he shattered both knees in competition. The road to recovery is sure to be long. But if he does make it to Beijing, he will no doubt make Canadians proud.

From Steve Bauer

Canada, being a hockey-mad winter-blown country, has never really been known for its cycling prowess. Since the first cycling races in the Olympics in 1896, Canadians have had only minor successes. The first cycling medal for Canada came in 1908 when the four-man team of William Anderson, Walter Andrews, Frederick McCarthy and William Morton won the bronze medal at the 1908 Olympics in London, England, in the team pursuit. It wasn't until 76 years later that a Canadian cyclist would once again stand atop an Olympic podium and see his nation's flag raised.

St. Catharines, Ontario, native Steve Bauer like most young Canadians only used his bike to get around the neighbourhood or down to the schoolyard to play some ball hockey. For him, a bike was simply a vehicle for getting around or occasionally racing his friends.

At 16 years old, since he was always beating his friends in races, he decided to give competitive cycling a try by joining the St. Catharines Cycling Club. He quickly found out that he was a natural at the sport, winning the 100-kilometre road race at the Ontario Summer Games.

Having just turned 18 years old, Bauer took his competitive nature to a new level and joined the Canadian National Cycling team competing in the team pursuit. With a face still marked by the occasional pimple, Bauer got his first few tastes of international competition. While still technically classified as a junior rider, he helped the Canadian men's team to a respectable 8th place finish at the Cycling World Championships in Venezuela in 1977.

After getting his first glimpse of the world of high stakes cycling, Bauer wanted to branch out his own and began a vigorous training program to improve his results. Soon, all the hard work began to pay off. He wanted to push to get into the 1980 Olympics, but Canada took part in the western boycott of the Games held in Communist Moscow that year.

Waiting patiently for the next Olympics, Bauer won a silver medal at the 1982 Commonwealth Games in the individual road race and a bronze medal at the 1984 World Championships in the Elite Men's Road Race. By the time the 1984 Olympics finally came around, Steve Bauer was considered as one of the top competitors in the individual road race and someone who could challenge for the gold.

But it wouldn't be easy. There was a long list of talented cyclists behind him all vying for that same spot. No Canadian had ever won a medal in the individual road race, so Bauer had no inspiration to draw upon or any teammates to support him during the gruelling 190-kilometre race. Not having any teammates meant that if one of the pack made a break for the lead, he would have to challenge each and every one.

Bauer remained at the head of the pack for the majority of the race along with three Americans and two Norwegians. With just 20 kilometres left in the race, American Alexi Grewal made a break for the finish line, pushing with all his power to put distance between Bauer and the others. By the 15-kilometre mark, Grewal had a 20-second lead on the closest cyclist and with every push of the pedal gained valuable time. It was now or never for Bauer, and he broke from the pack.

With only a few kilometres left in the race, Bauer had narrowed the gap and pulled within just a few feet of Grewal. It came down to a final sprint for the gold medal. Bauer was confident that Grewal had pushed himself too hard and had already used up his reserve energy. But Grewal was able to match Bauer through the final straightaway. The large crowd gathered around the finish line went into a frenzy as the two men came into sight. After 190-kilometre race, the pain was evident in the faces of both men as they focused on their goal just a few metres away. Despite Bauer's last minute heroics, the day belonged to the American Grewal, who just beat Bauer by half the length of a bicycle. Bauer had to settle for the silver medal. This was far from a disappointment. Bauer had taken Canadian cycling to a new level and had won a medal in an event that no Canadian had ever come close to winning.

Bauer turned professional after the Olympics and had a successful career racing in prestigious circuits like the Tour de France. In 1988 he became only the second Canadian to ever don the yellow jersey, holding onto it for five days.

In 1996, at the age of 37, Bauer decided to relive the glory days of the past and joined the Canadian team in Atlanta for the Olympics. But he was not that same cyclist who took home the silver 12 years earlier. He ended up coming 41st in the individual road race. His legend, however, will always live on as the first Canadian to win a medal in the individual road race.

Curtis Harnett: Cycling's Golden Boy

With his golden mane of curly hair, Curtis Harnett would have been the perfect spokesman for a shampoo company. He had the looks; he had the hair; he had the shine. But beyond all that, he also had three Olympic medals to his name.

Born in Toronto, Ontario, like most Canadian boys, he grew up playing hockey. After school and on weekends he was found on the street, at the outdoor arena or in a local rink working on his conditioning and his next great move. During the summer months, Harnett needed a way to stay in shape and chose cycling as the perfect exercise. To his surprise, he loved it. Quickly he realized that he would do a lot better in cycling than he would in hockey—an NHL player he was not—and so he made the switch into competitive cycling.

At just 17 years of age, Curtis Harnett jumped headfirst into cycling and began to make an impact immediately. After winning a few provincial and national races and only two years after entering the competitive world of cycling, Harnett found himself at the 1984 Olympic Games in Los Angeles, representing his country in the 1000-metre time trial event. Harnett's event was a race against the clock, a punishing discipline that pushed the athlete's legs to their limit over the 1000 metres of track. But Harnett loved the challenge, and in all probability enjoyed the pain because it was a sign that he was doing his best and pushing himself to the very limit. It was a sport of milliseconds so athletes had to forget about the pain because thinking about it could cost them valuable 10ths of a second.

Using his incredible leg muscles, Harnett pushed his bike to a second-place finish just .34 of a second behind the winner, West German Fredy Schimdtke. Harnett was just 19 years old, and he was on top of the world. But he wanted more. He wanted his hands on a gold medal. So, he set his sights on the 1988 Olympics in Seoul.

This time entering the Olympics in the match sprint event, Harnett rode to a disappointing 10th place finish. Harnett was not satisfied with that performance and vowed to return to the Olympics again for another chance at the gold medal.

At the 1992 Olympics in Barcelona, Curtis Harnett was back for a third time, ready to make a new push for gold. He had trained for the games intensely, and he would consider anything less than a gold or a silver a disappointment.

Harnett pushed himself to the limits and made it into the final sprints with German rider Jens Fiedler and Australian Gary Neiwand. But in the finals, Harnett just could not match the intense pace set by the powerful Europeans and lost his hopes of gold, settling for the bronze.

At 31 years of age Curtis Harnett returned to the Olympics in 1996. It would be his last chance at gold, for he said that these Games would be his last. In the 1000-metre sprint, he was up against his old rival and defending sprint gold medallist Jens Fiedler of Germany. It would not be easy to win gold. As predicted Harnett made his way through round after round and ended up in the finals. But Harnett would yet again have to watch from a distance as Jens Fiedler walked away with the gold medal. Harnett added another bronze medal to his collection. This time, the disappointment was as palpable as it was when he lost the gold in 1992. It was his last Games, and he loved every experience.

Harnett could not stay away from the Olympic Games completely. He returned in 2000 and 2004 as a cycling commentator for the CBC. He was also an instrumental part of Toronto's bid to host the 2008 Olympics. Today, he divides his time between various charities and public speaking events across Canada.

Canada's Baseball Surprise

Olympic baseball, since entering as a medal sport in 1992, has been dominated by a handful of countries that hang greedily onto their top spots. Countries like Cuba, Japan and the United States have consistently finished with a medal in each of the Olympics. The Cubans lead the way with three gold medals and one silver medal. Except for the Australian baseball team at the 2004 Olympics, no other team has been able to challenge the dominance of those three nations. But in 2004 one team surprised the world and made a few people nervous.

The Canadian team really came out of nowhere, surprising everyone simply by qualifying for the Olympics. The team was not filled with many names that people knew, but Canadian amateur baseball fans believed that they had a chance.

Led by the second baseman Richard "Stubby" Clapp, the Canadian team strung together a bunch of wins that placed them in serious contention for a medal. In the opening game, they steamrolled over Chinese Taipei winning the game 7–0. Decisive victories over the Italians and the Dutch followed. They would lose two games in a row to the superior Cuba and Japanese teams, but their record of 5–2 put them in third place. Canadian media flocked to find out the story of this Cinderella baseball team.

The Canadians defied all odds and made it into the semi-final round against the favourite Cubans. If they could beat the Cubans, the Canadian Baseball team surely would have been mentioned in the same breath as the American Olympic hockey team of 1980 that defeated the Russian in what is called the Miracle on Ice. Canada kept the game close with some ace pitching and excellent defence from all corners of the field. By the eighth inning, Canada was holding onto a slim lead of 3–2. The Canadians could not hold the Cubans back forever, and they rallied with six runs late in the game finally losing the game 8–5. There was a profound sense of disappointment on the Canadian's faces as the Cuban celebrated their advancement into the gold medal game.

Canada was left to battle it out for the bronze with the Japanese who had lost to the Australians. But history would not be made in that game as the Canadians were trounced by the Japanese with a score of 11–2 in the bronze medal game. Canada had to settle for fourth.

The Canadians did not disappoint in their run for the gold medal, and along the way won new fans around the world, even if they did miss becoming the top story in the Olympics by a few runs.

Quick Canadian Olympics Facts

- Lori-Ann Muenzer won the first-ever cycling Gold medal in woman's sprint at the Athens games.

- Kyle Shewfelt won Canada's first-ever gymnastics gold medal in artistic floor exercises at the 2004 Athens games.

- Clara Hughes won a bronze medal in the 5-kilometre speed-skating event in Salt Lake 2002 to add to the two bronze medals in cycling that she captured in the 1996 Atlanta Games. She becomes the first Canadian, the second woman and only the fourth person in Olympic history to capture medals in both the Summer and the Winter Games.

- Canada's best Olympic record performance ever was in the 1984 Summer Olympics at Los Angeles. The Canadians took home a total of 44 Medals: 10 gold, 18 silver and 16 bronze.

- At the 1976 Summer Games in Montréal, Canada, the host nation, failed to win a single gold medal, but took 5 silver and 6 bronze for a total of 11 medals.

- Canada did not compete in the first modern Olympics Games held in 1896 in Athens Greece.

- Lacrosse is Canada's national sport. So it is not surprising that the Shamrock Lacrosse Club out of Winnipeg easily won the gold medal at the 1904 St. Louis Olympics.

- When the Canadian men's lacrosse team captured the gold medal at the 1908 Olympics in London, England, they beat out a tough British opponent. That was Canada's only game because there were no other teams entered into the competition.

- Vancouver's Dave Steen won Canada's only decathlon medal of the century when he came in third place at the 1988 Olympics in Seoul, Korea. He was considered such a long shot to medal in the event that not one Canadian reporter was there to document the historical victory.

- Olympic trampoline athlete Karen Cockburn, bronze medallist at the 2000 Sydney Olympics, improved on her last results winning the silver medal at the 2004 Olympics in Athens.

- Torontonians John Child and Mark Hesse earned Canada a bronze medal in the new sport of beach volleyball at the 1996 Atlanta Games.

- Vancouver's Alison Sydor won a silver medal in the mountain bike race, a new medal sport at the 1996 Atlanta Games.

- Daniel Nestor and Sebastien Lareau were ranked fourth in the world in doubles tennis before the start of the 2000 Olympics in Sydney, Australia.

- Nestor and Lareau made it into the final match for the gold medal against the world's number one team and local favourites, the Australians Mark Woodforde and Todd Woodbridge. Nestor and Lareau managed to shake off the partisan crowd and defeat the Aussies for the gold. That gold is Canada's only tennis medal in Olympic history...so far.

- Women's basketball became an official sport at the 1976 Olympics in Montréal.

- The 1976 Olympics in Montréal was the first time events were televised live.

- The 1924 Olympics in Paris, proved a disappointment for the Canadians, it was the first time that Canada did not win an Olympic gold. But this unpleasant fact isn't unique. Canada went gold-less at the 1948, 1960, 1972 and 1976 Olympics.

- Canadian pop singer Avril Lavigne contributed a song called "Unity" for the official album of the 2004 Athens Olympics.

The Stats

Canada's Olympic Medals
1900–2004

Year	Location	Gold	Silver	Bronze	Total	# of Athletes
1900	Paris, France	1	0	1	2	2
1904	St. Louis, U.S.A.	4	1	1	6	43
1906	Athens, Greece	1	1	0	2	4
1908	London, England	3	3	9	15	91
1912	Stockholm, Sweden	3	2	2	7	36
1916	Cancelled due to WWI	N/A	N/A	N/A	N/A	N/A
1920	Antwerp, Belgium	3	3	3	9	47
1924	Paris, France	0	3	1	4	73
1928	Amsterdam, Netherlands	4	4	7	15	71
1932	Los Angeles, U.S.A.	2	5	8	15	102

Canada's Olympic Medals, cont.

Year	Location	Gold	Silver	Bronze	Total	# of Athletes
1936	Berlin, Germany	1	3	5	9	109
1940	Cancelled due to WWII	N/A	N/A	N/A	N/A	N/A
1944	Cancelled due to WWII	N/A	N/A	N/A	N/A	N/A
1948	London, England	0	1	2	3	106
1952	Helsinki, Finland	1	2	0	3	113
1956	Melbourne, Australia	2	1	3	6	99
1960	Rome, Italy	0	1	0	1	97
1964	Tokyo, Japan	1	2	1	4	118
1968	Mexico City, Mexico	1	3	1	5	143
1972	Munich, Germany	0	2	3	5	220
1976	Montreal, Canada	0	5	6	11	414
1980	Moscow, Soviet Union (Boycotted)	0	0	0	0	0
1984	Los Angeles, U.S.A.	10	18	16	44	436
1988	Seoul, Korea	3	2	5	10	354
1992	Barcelona, Spain	7	4	7	18	314
1996	Atlanta, U.S.A.	3	11	8	22	307
2000	Sydney, Australia	3	3	8	14	311
2004	Athens, Greece	3	6	3	12	345
Totals		56	86	100	242	4176

Canada's Olympic Medal Summary by Sport

Sport	Gold	Silver	Bronze
Art contest	0	1	1
Basketball	0	1	0
Boxing	3	7	7
Canoeing	4	8	7
Cycling	1	5	5
Diving	1	2	4
Equestrian	1	1	2
Golf	1	0	0
Gymnastics	2	1	2
Ice Hockey	1	0	0
Judo	0	2	2
Lacrosse	2	0	2
Rowing	8	13	12
Sailing	0	3	6
Shooting	4	3	2
Soccer	1	0	0
Swimming	7	13	18
Synchronized Swimming	3	4	1
Tennis	1	0	0
Taekwondo	0	0	1
Triathlon	1	0	0
Volleyball	0	0	1
Weightlifting	0	2	0
Wrestling	1	6	5
Totals	55	87	98

Notes on Sources

Beddoes, Dick, Jim Coleman, et al. *Winners: A Century of Canadian Sport.* Toronto: Canadian Press, 1985.

Best, Dave ed. *Canada: Our Century in Sport.* Markham: Fitzhenry & Whiteside, 2002.

Howell, Nancy and Maxwell, Howell. *Sports and Games in Canadian Life.* Toronto: Macmillan of Canada, 1969.

Kelley, Malcolm G. *Canadian Sports History and Trivia.* Scarborough, Prentice Hall Canada, 2004.

McDonald, David and Lauren Drewery. *For the Record: Canada's Greatest Women Athletes.* Mesa Associates, 1981.

Mednick, Robin & Wendy Thomas. *Heroes in Our Midst. Top Canadian Athletes Share their Personal Stories from their Lives in Sport.* Toronto: McClelland & Stewart Ltd, 2001.

Podnieks, Andrew. *Canada's Olympic Hockey Teams: The Complete History.* Toronto, Doubleday Canada, 1997.

Wallechinsky, David. *The Complete Book of the Winter Olympics.* Little, Brown and Company, 1994.

Web Sources

http://www.cbc.ca/sports/

http://www.ctv.ca/

http://gymn.ca/athletes/

http://www.i-needtoknow.com/kyle/

http://www.theglobeandmail.com/

http://www.chantalpetitclerc.com/2003-2004/

http://www.cshof.ca/

http://www.rickhansen.com/

http://www.stevebauer.com/

http://archives.cbc.ca/

http://www.curtharnett.ca/

J. Alexander Poulton

J. Alexander Poulton is a writer, photographer and genuine Canadian sports enthusiast. A resident of Montreal all his life, he has been known to "call in sick" during the Olympics broadcast so that he can get as much viewing in as possible.

He earned his B.A in English Literature from McGill University and his graduate diploma in Journalism from Concordia University. He has 10 other sports books to his credit, including books on hockey, soccer, and baseball.

MORE GREAT TITLES FROM OVERTIME BOOKS...

GREATEST MOMENTS IN CANADIAN HOCKEY
by J. Alexander Poulton

A fan—tastic collection of stories about the players, teams, coaches and moments that changed the game forever. These memorable highlights stand out as significant markers in the history of Canadian hockey.

$9.95 • ISBN 978-0-9737681-4-5 • 144 pages

CANADIAN HOCKEY RECORD BREAKERS
Legendary Feats by Canada's Greatest Players
by J. Alexander Poulton

Which Canadian hockey player scored the most goals in his NHL career? Which goaltender racked up the most shut-outs? Who was the first woman to register a point in a professional men's hockey game? This new book answers these hockey trivia questions and many more.

$9.95 • ISBN 978-0-9737681-0-7 • 144 pages

HOCKEY'S HOTTEST PLAYERS
The On- & Off- Ice Stories of the Superstars
by Arpon Basu

Sports journalist Arpon Basu profiles today's rising stars in the National Hockey League. He looks not only at their on-ice performance and statistics but also probes the human story behind their victories and struggles, revealing the journey they've taken to reach the highest echelons of their sport.

$9.95 • ISBN 978-0-9737681-3-8 • 144 pages

WEIRD FACTS ABOUT CANADIAN HOCKEY
Strange, Wacky & Hilarious Stories
by Peter Boer

Hockey, our national sport, is played everywhere from urban cul-de-sacs to NHL arenas. Games are rife with tales of the odd, the strange, the funny and, occasionally, the disturbing side of hockey history.

$9.95 • ISBN 978-0-9737681-2-1 • 160 pages

WORLD'S GREATEST SOCCER PLAYERS
by J. Alexander Poulton

Soccer is the world's most-watched sport, and these are the world's favorite players. From David Beckham, the celebrity midfielder, to Thierry Henry, who made his way from a Parisian ghetto to the top of soccer fame and many more, read the stories of the greatest players on the field today.

$9.95 • ISBN 978-0-9737681-9-0 • 144 pages

OverTime Books has titles covering a wide range of sports. Look for our books at your local bookseller and newsstand or contact our distributor directly, Lone Pine Publishing. In the U.S. call 1-800-518-3541. In Canada, call 1-800-661-9017.

AT OVERTIME BOOKS...
WE'RE CRAZY ABOUT SPORTS!

If you enjoyed *Canadians at the Summer Olympics*, check out more 2008 titles...